MORE IN THE SERIES

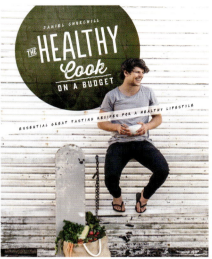

COMING SOON

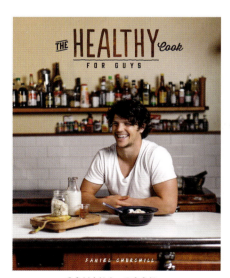

COMING SOON

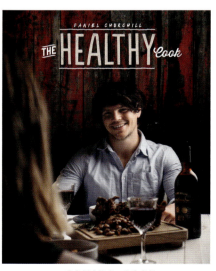

COMING SOON

THE HEALTHY Cook

DAN CHURCHILL

ART DIRECTOR
JAY BEAUMONT

PHOTOGRAPHY
MICHAEL MARCHMENT

STYLING
MADI COPPOCK

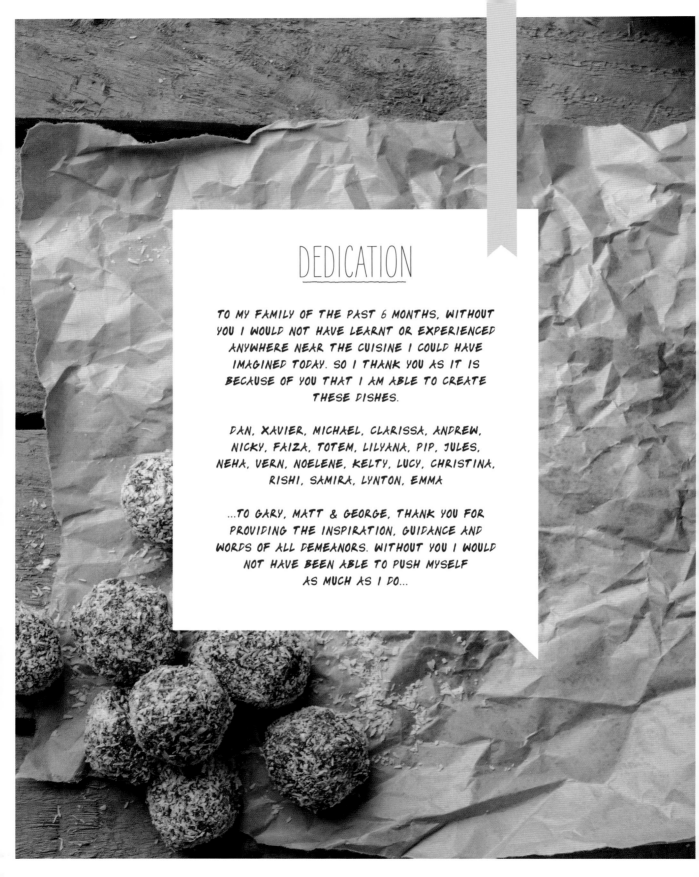

DEDICATION

TO MY FAMILY OF THE PAST 6 MONTHS, WITHOUT YOU I WOULD NOT HAVE LEARNT OR EXPERIENCED ANYWHERE NEAR THE CUISINE I COULD HAVE IMAGINED TODAY. SO I THANK YOU AS IT IS BECAUSE OF YOU THAT I AM ABLE TO CREATE THESE DISHES.

DAN, XAVIER, MICHAEL, CLARISSA, ANDREW, NICKY, FAIZA, TOTEM, LILYANA, PIP, JULES, NEHA, VERN, NOELENE, KELTY, LUCY, CHRISTINA, RISHI, SAMIRA, LYNTON, EMMA

...TO GARY, MATT & GEORGE, THANK YOU FOR PROVIDING THE INSPIRATION, GUIDANCE AND WORDS OF ALL DEMEANORS. WITHOUT YOU I WOULD NOT HAVE BEEN ABLE TO PUSH MYSELF AS MUCH AS I DO...

THE HEALTHY COOK

CONTENTS

THE BASICS

Onion Rings 20
Mayonnaise 22
Kale Chips 24
Fish Stock 26
Chicken Stock 28
Sweet Potato Gnocchi 30

BREAKFAST

Bircher with Zesty Raspberry Sauce 36
Choc Banana Protein Shake 38
My Breakfast Frittata 40
Breakfast Smoothie 42
Corn Fritters with Avocado Salsa 44
My Homemade Granola 46
Fruit Smoothie 48
Sweet Potato Fritters with Chilli Tomato Jam 50
Green Smoothie 52

MEAT DISHES

Smoky Chicken Legs 58
Pull Apart Lamb with Roasted Butter Beans 60
Eye Fillet Steak with Salsa Verde 62
Green Masala 66
Butterflied Lamb in a Middle Eastern Rub 68
Chicken Parmy 70
Lamb Cutlets with Macadamia Crust 72
Mustard and Peppercorn Roo 76
Country Chicken Sweet Potato Top Pie 78
Juicy Chicken Breast with Roast Pumpkin 80
Beef Tortillas with Kale Slaw 82
Sesame Satay Skewers 86

SEAFOOD

Bouillabaisse 92
Poached Salmon in a Walnut Apple Salad 94
Crispy Skin Salmon and Three Grain Salad 96
Whole Snapper in a Tamarind Sauce 100
Mussels in White Wine 102
Prawn & Apple Rice Paper Rolls 104
Seared Scallops with Apple and Fennel Salad ... 108
Oven Baked Trout 110
Tuna Buckwheat Tabbouleh 112
Seafood Marinara with Sweet Potato Gnocchi ... 114
Snapper with Creole Sauce 118

VEGETARIAN

Broccoli Pesto Quinoa Salad 124
Ricotta, Beetroot and Zucchini Slice 126
Italian Quinoa Salad with Basil Oil 128
Tofu, Buckwheat and Chickpea Salad 130
Sweet Potato Rosti 132
Beetroot and Sweet Potato Chips 134

CHEATING

Coconut Milk Coco 140
Buckwheat Pancakes 142
Protein Balls 144
Sweet Strawberry and Coconut Muffins 146
Homemade Tortillas & Tostadas 148
Flourless Banana Bread 150

INDEX 152

MY PHILOSOPHY

MY PASSION AND PHILOSOPHY FOR WHAT FOOD BRINGS TO AN INDIVIDUAL... HAPPINESS.

How often do you find yourself grumpy or angry because you are starving? How much do you love going out to dinner, lunch or breakfast? How good is the feeling when your big plate of food arrives in front of you with the smell going straight into your nostrils? Sound familiar?

It is through this passion and love for food that we get a true rush of happiness thanks to the relationship with our hormones. By eating, you create a sense of enjoyment and this is well supported by the release of endorphins and serotonin from your glands.

In my opinion some of the best times of the day revolve around our food. By sitting down to eat you are encouraged to create conversation. It is through this that better relationships are formed and you get to find out what your friends and family were involved in throughout their day. In a way family relationships can be enhanced based on meal times as they are a part of the day when everyone shuts off from work and other distractions and just listens to one another. In a time where life is so busy and family can often be neglected, it is so important to just slow down and enjoy great company from those who mean the most to you.
Thank God for food.

DOWNLOAD THE LAYAR APP ON YOUR SMARTPHONE OR TABLET TO WATCH HOW TO VIDEOS IN MY COOK BOOK

LOOK FOR
THIS ICON

INTRODUCTION

ABOUT THE HEALTHY COOK

When asked how I began my cooking journey many are surprised to hear that I wasn't heavily taught by either of my parents. This is not to say they did not have a major influence in my cooking direction. When I was about 12 years old my family and I would love to sit down to watch Jamie Oliver do his thing on TV. It was one of our favourite times of the week as we watched in anticipation at the way he made meals easy. Through this, dad developed a pretty cool system. On a Sunday he would bring out the pen and paper and mark up the 'Churchill Family Cooking Roster.' We would literally 'shotgun' a night during the week that suited us to prepare and cook dinner for the rest of the family. The early days were pretty interesting. I remember watching the rest of the family try and swallow and pretend to enjoy some of the dishes that I had attempted to put together. But as the roster continued to be a ritual my skills grew. I began to challenge myself with more technical dishes and my determination to perform was always at the forefront of my mind.

Growing up with a family of two brothers, sport was always a major point of conversation over dinner. Every weekend mum and dad would work out car pools to get us around to rugby matches and make sure their weekend wasn't much more than a taxi service. But it was this sibling rivalry that generated a love for health and fitness. I remember when Brendan said I wouldn't be able to do a 10 minute plank and so naturally I went out and did it. I guess it just shows our family's competitiveness.

It wasn't until my early 20's that I fully grasped how much I had learnt about food by just cooking from week to week. With my mates learning of my passion it wasn't too long before they were asking for advice on how to cook to impress a special girl. It was from these scenarios that I ended up self publishing my first cookbook DudeFood Volume 1. This was just the beginning. I completed a Master in Exercise Science, ran my own health coach and fitness business and wanted to educate more people to achieve long lasting, sustainable and healthy lifestyles. I found too many people considered healthy living unachievable and I wanted to demonstrate this is not the case. All you need is a little push and some helpful direction and this is the reason I came up with The Healthy Cook.

WHAT TO EXPECT

The Healthy Cook is set to revolutionise the way you look at healthy cooking, being one of the first cookbooks to provide the macronutrient (Protein, Fats and Carbohydrates) information for each meal, all in a simple table. Readers will learn about what they are actually digesting just from a quick glance. An efficient and easy way to understand how balanced your meals really are.

The Healthy Cook also incorporates the use of an easy to read slide bar including the aspects of time, skill and health. Rather than looking though the ingredients to determine if the recipe is right for tonight's dinner, within seconds you will be able to make a decision on what to cook based on your skill set, how healthy you want your dish to be and how much time you have. A simple tool which is going to reshape how you look at a cookbook. No more flicking aimlessly through recipes waisting time trying to get the perfect dish for the occasion, you can make that decision within seconds.

The Healthy Cook is truly ahead of its time. In order to really engage the audience readers are also given the opportunity to cook with me in your own home thanks to the virtual response application in Layar. By downloading this free application readers will be able to hover over the pages and gain a virtual insight into cooking techniques and methods. By simply downloading Layar from the app or play store you will also unlock more tips and insights into food and nutrition. At this point, I would like to formally thank you for inviting me into your kitchen and I look forward to hearing about your cooking journey. Let your new experience on healthy cooking begin.

NUTRITION TABLE

The nutrition tables used throughout the book should be referred to as a guide. Given the variance in produce they have been calculated off their normative values and therefore would not be consistently accurate once the dish is replicated.

HEALTHY INSIGHTS

BEING HEALTHY IS A LIFESTYLE CHOICE, AND IT DOESN'T MEAN YOU HAVE TO SACRIFICE GREAT TASTE. THESE SIMPLE INSIGHTS WILL GIVE A UNDERSTANDING INTO HOW TO MAKE SOME VERY SIMPLE CHANGES TO BE THAT BIT HEALTHIER.

WHAT ARE PROTEINS, FATS AND CARBS?

Every individual is different and because of this our intakes vary. As a result there is no set figure for you to try to achieve when reading the nutritional tables. Instead they are there to educate you on what you are putting into your body. It's not there to live your life by, I never want you to have the added stress of working with figures to enjoy your meals. If you do need a bit of guidance work off ratios. For me, my macronutrients consist of 40% Protein, 30% Fat, 30% Carbohydrates. Again, this is not something I worked out, I simply look at my plate and have a general understanding. This way there is more time for my brain to concentrate on food and less time for figures.

PROTEIN

A fundamental building block for muscular repair and adaptation. Through its regular consumption it also aids in brain function. With a strong source of fibre it is great for digestion. There are a number of ways to get protein throughout the day and the best is through natural sources such as meat and legumes. You can also reach out to sources such as protein powder which are very efficient and convenient, particularly after a workout where intake is pivotal. However these are sources that you shouldn't become reliant on as it deters your body from doing what it was built for and breaking down nutrients for fuel.

FAT

We often mistake these for a poor nutrient, something that harms the body and does nothing but insulate us over winter. This is, however, a misconception. Due to an analysis performed in the 1950's, the perception of fats would be set on a misleading tangent for many decades. Quality fats are essential to the body, they aid in brain function, weight loss, healthy cholesterol levels, immune function, repair and growth of damaged tissue, skin and eye care and the list goes on. Our cells are predominantly made up of fat and therefore we must be consuming it within our meals to ensure we can maintain a healthy body and mind. It is important to note that there are bad fats and these are the ones to avoid. The two main types of fats are unsaturated and saturated. Generally you want to be avoiding saturated fats which generate a lot of artery clogging and lifestyle diseases. However, there are a few saturated fats such as that found in coconut milk that are amazing, particularly for your immune system. I include coconut milk on average a couple of times per week and cook quite often with coconut oil. Unsaturated fats are made up of monounsaturated and polyunsaturated which you will find in olive oils, nuts, seeds and oily fish respectively.

When viewing the nutrition table you will observe total fats and saturated fats in brackets. Most of the time you want the saturated fats to be quite minimal, but you will notice in the recipes including coconut milk they are a bit higher than usual.

CARBOHYDRATES

These are a great source of energy and are present in almost every food. Similar to fats, carbohydrates contain both good and bad sources. Believe it or not vegetables are the best source of carbohydrates as they are low in sugar and contain a number of micronutrients to help you throughout the day. Fruits are also great, although they contain a little more sugar but offer a range of essential minerals. Avoid heavily starched carbohydrates as they contain minimal nutritional content. These include wheat based products such as pasta, pizza and bread. One way to avoid these are to simply take note of colour. More often than not, poor nutrient based carbohydrates are white or creamy in colour. If you compare that to the range of vegetables and fruit then it is an easy way to walk through your isles and distinguish between the two. Throughout this book you will see a range of colours showcasing the beauty of our healthy and quality produce.

COOKING WITH OILS

THERE ARE A NUMBER OF OILS YOU CAN COOK WITH THAT HAVE DIFFERING DEPTHS OF FLAVOUR AND QUALITY OF FATS. BUT BECAUSE THERE ARE SO MANY, IT'S HARD TO UNDERSTAND WHICH ONES ARE BEST FOR PARTICULAR COOKING OCCASIONS. OLIVE OIL EVEN HAS A FEW WITHIN ITSELF.

EXTRA VIRGIN OLIVE OIL

This is the first press from the olives. It offers the greatest amount of quality fat and is therefore one of the best for you. It is dark in colour and has a strong flavour and is more ideal for finishing in salads rather than sauces such as mayonnaise as the taste overpowers other ingredients. Extra Virgin also has a very low smoking point, so if you are using heat it can result in burning whatever it is you are cooking.

PURE OLIVE OIL

This is the second press from the olives and as a result does not have as many quality fats. It is lighter in colour and has a higher smoking point than Extra Virgin so I recommend using this oil to cook with when using heat. It also has a more reasonable use in sauces due to its non-impeding flavour.

LIGHT OLIVE OIL

This is the final press one can manage to get out of the olives. Manufacturers actually heat the press in an attempt to extract as much 'juice' out of what is apparently left in the crushed olive. Along with this, a lot of manufacturers will add ingredients to enhance the oil's flavour as it is quite weak. It has a really light colour and I recommend avoiding this altogether.

GRAPESEED OIL

I love using this to cook when working with heat. It has a really high smoking point and therefore will not result in your food becoming charcoal quickly. If you really want the taste of your sauces to shine, grapeseed's flavour is next to none. Apart from finishing in salads, grapeseed oil is one of the most common I use.

MACADAMIA OIL

I love this oil for the nuttiness it provides to dishes. It also has a high smoking point and so it is great for cooking with heat. I have become very fond of infusing this oil with flavours such as chilli, garlic and herbs. It takes on flavour really well whilst still holding its own.

COCONUT OIL

Similar to macadamia oil, coconut oil provides a great nuttiness to your cooking. It is extremely healthy for you as the fat included in this oil is not only amazing for you heart, but also for your brain. As coconut oil is a Medium Chain Fatty Acid (MCFA) it is regarded as a healthy saturated fat. It is broken down in the liver and converted to energy for the brain and muscular function. I use it a lot in Indian cooking due to the way it compliments coconut milk and spices. I have become accustomed to using it in a number of baking dishes too due to its similar consistency to butter. I substitute a lot of recipes that include butter with coconut oil purely because it gets the same moist result, and in my opinion tastes even better.

HEALTHY INSIGHTS

ALMOND MILK

ALTHOUGH I LOVE MY MILK, MOST PEOPLE UNFORTUNATELY INCLUDE TOO MUCH DAIRY IN THEIR DIET. DAIRY PRODUCTS ARE AWESOME AND CAN BE USED IN SO MANY CUISINES. YOGHURT FOR MARINADES OR BREAKFAST OPTIONS, MILK FOR SMOOTHIES AND PANCAKES AND YOU CAN'T FORGET CREAM FOR SOUPS, DESSERTS AND SAUCES.

The problem lies in "too much is not a good thing." Although dairy products offer amazing vitamins and minerals, such as the obvious – calcium for bones, muscular and brain function, unfortunately it also contains high levels of acidity.

Your body is an amazing system. When your body has too much of one thing it will create ways to balance it out. In this case, when your body has too much acidity due to dairy it will excrete most of it out through your urine. Although this sounds like a good thing, when you do go to the toilet you also lose all the amazing nutrients present within the food. So, although dairy is high in calcium, you may not absorb much of it as it is aligned with high acidity levels.

This became a problem for me because I love my smoothies. However I learned to combat it by creating my very own Almond milk. Although it doesn't have as much calcium compared to cow's milk, almond milk has plenty of antioxidants and, after being soaked, is great for stomach digestion, not to mention how it lowers cholesterol levels with its amazing quality fat. To make the base of almond milk all you need is almonds and water. From there you can vary and come up with your own mix. Commercial brands tend to add confectionary sugar, I personally don't think it is necessary, but it's up to you.

INGREDIENTS

1 cup almonds

700ml water, plus extra for soaking

METHOD

Cover the almonds with water in a bowl and allow them to soak overnight.

The next day boil 700ml of water and allow to cool slightly.

Drain the almonds and then blend with the hot water until liquified.

Pass through a fine sieve, As it cools the mixture will thicken slightly.

HEALTHY INSIGHTS

CAN THE TOMATOES

Fruit in tins are usually bad enough purely because they are created for the purpose of longevity. Not only do they contain additional sugars and preservatives to enhance flavour but also colouring agents because over time they lose their natural quality.

Tinned tomatoes are even worse, but this is not because manufacturers pack even more harmful products into the cylinder frame, rather the reason lies within the tomatoes themselves. Tomatoes contain a high element of acidity which after remaining inside a tin for a period of time actually breaks down the aluminum of the tin itself. Once broken down it then moves freely within the tin which means when you use it in your meals you are adding elements of metal to your food too. Unless you have toxins on your ingredients list it's probably best you try to avoid the tin altogether. Simply get four tomatoes and put them in a blender. Pulse until you get the consistency you're after – short time for chunky or a longer time for smooth.

SHOULD WE BE HAVING BREAD?

IN SHORT THE ANSWER IS NO. OUR BODIES WERE NOT CREATED TO DIGEST WHAT MAKES UP THE DOUGH.

Our stomach struggles to comfortably break down the combination of gluten and yeast and this is why some people unfortunately do not feel great after having a sandwich over lunch. Many dietary issues have resulted in people being diagnosed with coeliac disease, resulting in a gluten free diet.

Gluten is found in wheat related products such as flour, barley and rye and it is responsible for the stretchy aspect of pizza dough, pasta and bread. It is this glue like character that is the problem for the body's internal state to breakdown.

As bread in the modern age is a big part of meals in western society, to some degree our bodies are becoming adaptable to breaking it down. As a result, the onset of the associated illnesses are being delayed and individuals are not being affected until their early twenties.

Symptoms can include headaches, nausea, swelling and distal joints all being more common in women. I was able to understand the situation when I was a teenager as my mum unfortunately has been affected by it. So I learned to always either accommodate for her, or just change the meal altogether to avoid the consumption of gluten.

Pastas also include a high level of gluten and do not offer a lot of nutritional benefits. The Healthy Cook demonstrates how you can create a number of meals without getting caught up in bread and pasta.

As always, I say "everything in moderation is so important for your health." My spaghetti bolognaise is something I can't be without and as I love Italy, I obviously love my pasta and pizza. I do not have them too often, but I still do have them. If you can tolerate gluten, learn to know how much is enough for yourself. I still have bread once every three weeks as I have realised it is not something I need.

THE BASICS

IN MY EYES THESE ARE YOUR COOKING 101'S THAT YOU SHOULD ALWAYS HAVE UP YOUR SLEEVE. ONCE YOU HAVE BECOME ACCOMPLISHED AT THEM THEY OPEN THE DOOR TO SO MANY DISHES AND ACCOMPANIMENTS. BUT BEING BASIC DOES NOT MEAN THEY ARE NOT TASTY...

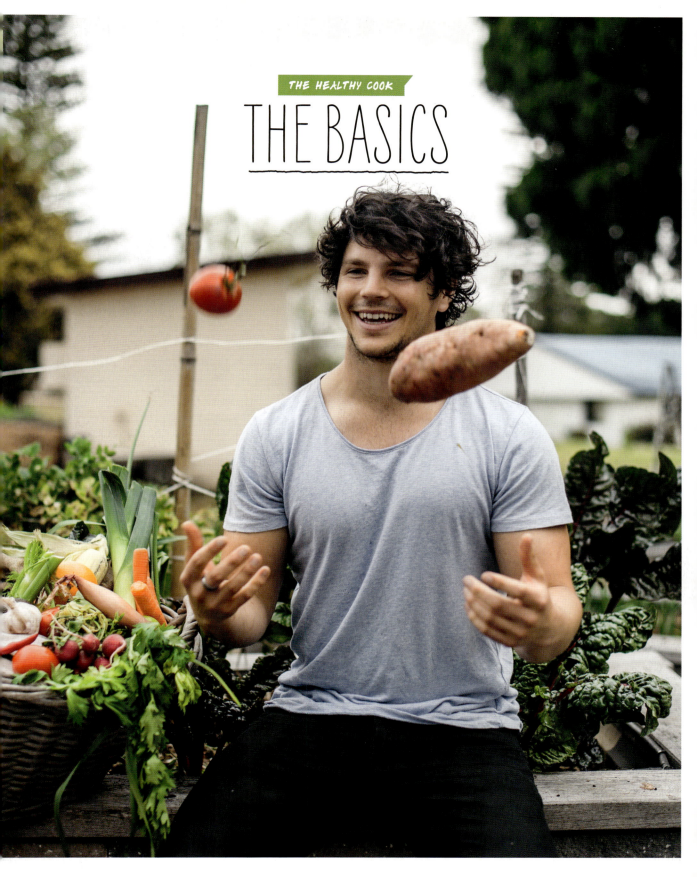

THE HEALTHY COOK

THE BASICS

ONION RINGS

IF I EVER HAVE A CHIP CRAVING, ALONG WITH KALE CHIPS, THESE ONION RINGS SERIOUSLY SATISFY THAT URGE. THEY HAVE A BETTER ROBUST FLAVOUR AND DON'T HAVE THAT SAME OILY FINISH COMPARED TO THE GLUTEN BASED ONES FOUND AT THE LOCAL BURGER JOINTS.

INGREDIENTS

1 onion, peeled and sliced

½ cup almond meal

Ice cubes

3 eggs

1 cup soda water

Spice mix

Salt

1 tbsp paprika

2 tsp cayenne pepper

1 tbsp white pepper, ground

METHOD

Whisk the eggs then add in the flour, soda water, pinch salt and ice cubes. Continue whisking to ensure sediment doesn't fall to the bottom.

Separate each slice of onion to make rings.

Combine spice mix and set aside.

In a medium saucepan heat the oil to 180°C.

Once the oil is hot enough, using tongs, or if you can chopsticks, dip an onion ring into the batter, lift out allowing excess mix to drip off and add straight to the saucepan. Cook until golden brown. Remove onto paper towel and immediately dust over spice mix. Repeat with remaining onions.

SNAPSHOT   SERVES: 4

- TIME
- HEALTHY
- SKILL

PROTEIN	FATS	CARBS
8g	11.4g (1.6g) saturated	2.8g (2.2g) sugars

per serve

MAYONNAISE

ALTHOUGH MAYONNAISE CONTAINS A HIGH LEVEL OF FAT, IF YOU MAKE YOUR OWN MAYONNAISE AND LEARN TO HAVE IT IN MODERATION ;) IT'S NOT THAT BAD FOR YOU. BUT THE BIGGEST ADVANTAGE IS THAT IT ACTS AS A BASE TO SO MANY SAUCE OPTIONS. SIMPLY ADD CHILLI AND PAPRIKA FOR SMOKINESS OR EGGS, GHERKINS AND CORNICHONS FOR A GREBICHE. THE POSSIBILITIES ARE ENDLESS.

INGREDIENTS

- 2 egg yolks
- 1 tbsp Dijon mustard
- Pinch of salt
- 100ml grapeseed or pure olive oil
- Juice of ½ lemon

METHOD

In a bowl combine the egg yolks, mustard and salt.

Add a tiny amount of oil and whisk until it is combined.

Then start to stream in more small amounts of oil, again, whisking it all the way in until there is no more oil remaining. The mixture should be thick and slightly hang from the whisk before dropping when held up.

Finish by squeezing in the lemon juice and a pinch of salt if needed.

SNAPSHOT

SERVES: **4**

PROTEIN	FATS	CARBS
6.3g	30g (4.4g) saturated	1.1g (1.1g) sugars

per serve

KALE CHIPS

I THINK THIS WOULD HAVE TO BE ONE OF MY FAVOURITE SNACKS TO MAKE. THE IDEA BEHIND SOMETHING CRUNCHY AND HOT WITHOUT THE STARCH IS SO SATISFYING. ONE OF THE BEST THINGS ABOUT THESE CHIPS IS HOW LITTLE TIME THEY TAKE TO CREATE.

INGREDIENTS

1 bunch of fresh kale

1 tbsp olive oil

Pinch of salt

METHOD

Preheat the oven to 180°C.

Carefully tear the leaves of kale into a mixing bowl.

Drizzle over the oil and carefully toss through the kale.

Lay out onto a lined baking tray and sprinkle with salt, then cook for 8 - 10 minutes.

VARIATIONS

Lemon Salt
Zest of 1 whole lemon
2 good pinches of salt

Spicy
1 tsp cayenne pepper
2 tsp paprika

Lemongrass, Ginger & Honey
1 lemon grass stalk, finely chopped
2 tsp honey
½ knob of ginger, finely chopped

SNAPSHOT

SERVES: **4**

- TIME
- HEALTHY
- SKILL

PROTEIN	FATS	CARBS
1.6g	8.2g (1.3g) saturated	2.1g (2.1g) sugars

per serve

watch me make this fish stock

FISH STOCK

I don't know how to further endorse making your own fish stock. It tastes that much cleaner. And unlike other stocks, a fish stock should only be cooked for 25-30 minutes, otherwise the bones develop a really bitter taste. This is because all of their flavour has been absorbed.

INGREDIENTS

Fish bones

1 onion, sliced

1 fennel bulb, sliced

1 celery stick, sliced

2 tsp fennel seeds

1 bay leaf

½ handful of parsley, roughly chopped

¼ cup white wine vinegar

1 good pinch of salt

METHOD

Remove eyeballs from fish and rinse bones and head under cold water to remove the blood and gunk. Chop into pieces so that it fits inside the saucepan.

Add the bones, onion, fennel bulb, celery, fennel seeds and bay leaf to the pot. Add enough water to cover all ingredients and place on the stove on high heat. Bring to the boil then reduce to low and add the parsley, white wine, vinegar and salt. Cover and allow to simmer for 20 minutes.

Pass through a sieve and divide into 250ml portions into plastic or tupperware containers. Store in the freezer and reheat when needed.

SNAPSHOT

SERVES: **4**

PROTEIN	FATS	CARBS
6.9g	3.2g (1.2g) saturated	1.0g (1.0g) sugars

per serve

THE BASICS

CHICKEN STOCK

HOW OFTEN HAVE YOU THROWN YOUR BONES INTO THE BIN AFTER A ROAST OR AFTER DE-BONING A CHICKEN? RATHER THAN WASTING THEIR AMAZING FLAVOUR AND NUTRIENTS USE THEM TO CREATE A STOCK OF YOUR OWN. YOU REALLY DON'T DO ANYTHING BUT PUT A POT ON THE STOVE WITH THE BELOW INGREDIENTS AND ALLOW IT TO DO ITS THING. THE LONGER YOU LEAVE IT THE BETTER.

INGREDIENTS

- 1 chicken carcass
- 1 tbsp olive oil
- 1 onion, sliced
- 1 carrot, sliced
- 1 celery, sliced
- 2 garlic cloves, crushed
- 2 bay Leaves
- 1 tbsp black peppercorns
- 3 sprigs of thyme
- 1 sprig rosemary
- 2 good pinches of salt

METHOD

Break up the carcass with a knife so that the bones will fit inside a stock pot. This will also extract more flavour with more surface area exposed.

Heat the oil in a big saucepan on medium to high heat. Add the chicken and brown all over.

Add the onion, celery, carrot and garlic. Fill with 2L of water and turn the temperature to high. Bring to a boil and then turn to low. Add the bay leaves, peppercorns, thyme, rosemary and salt. Cover and allow to simmer for a minimum of 12 hours. Ideally the longer the better as more flavour is extracted from the ingredients.

Pass stock through a sieve and pour into 250ml plastic containers. Place in the freezer and reheat when needed.

SNAPSHOT   SERVES: 5

- TIME
- HEALTHY
- SKILL

PROTEIN	FATS	CARBS
9.5g	4.1g (0.9g) saturated	1.4g (0.9g) sugars

per serve

SWEET POTATO GNOCCHI

I LOVE MAKING THESE, POACHING THEM AND STORING THEM IN THE FRIDGE FOR THE WEEK. ALL I HAVE TO DO IS FINISH THEM OFF IN THE PAN UNTIL THEY GET A GOLDEN CRUST. IT CAN TAKE PRACTICE, BUT ONCE YOU NAIL THEM ITS AMAZING BITING INTO THE CRISPY CASING SURROUNDING A LITTLE POCKET FULL OF SOFT SWEET POTATO.

INGREDIENTS

Gnocchi

- 1 large sweet potato, peeled & cubed
- 1 cup buckwheat flour
- 1 tsp salt
- 1 egg yolk
- 1 tbsp olive oil

METHOD

Preheat oven to 180°C.

Bring a pot of water to the boil, add the salt along with the potato, then turn heat to medium and allow to cook for 10 - 12 minutes, or until a knife penetrates easily. Drain through a colander and let stand for 5 minutes to release as much moisture as possible.

Line a baking tray with baking paper and spread potato over it. Place in the oven to further dry our for 8 minutes, making sure they do not change colour.

Remove from the oven and pass through a sieve or a ricer. If you don't have either you can just use the back of a fork in a mixing bowl.

Add the yolk and half the flour and begin to combine the mixture into a dough. Gradually add the flour until you reach a strong dough consistency.

Bring a pot of water to the boil and drop a little portion of the dough into it. If it separates you will need to add more flour. If it doesn't you are right to continue.

Divide dough into quarters and then roll each in the shape of a snake on the bench to a consistent 1cm thickness. Using a knife divide the length into 11 x 2 cm portions.

Bring the pot of water back up to the boil, then turn the heat to medium and add the gnocchi in portions as to not overcrowd the pan. Cook for 90 seconds before removing onto a paper towel. Repeat with remaining gnocchi.

Add 1 tbsp of oil to a frypan on high heat and cook gnocchi on each side for 1 - 2 minutes or until golden and crispy. Set aside to serve.

Note: To get a cool pattern on the gnocchi, once divided into portions roll them down a downward facing fork. This will give them line indents which look great for presentation.

SNAPSHOT

SERVES: **4**

- TIME
- HEALTHY
- SKILL

PROTEIN	FATS	CARBS
6.9g	3.2g (1.2g) saturated	1.0g (1.0g) sugars

per serve

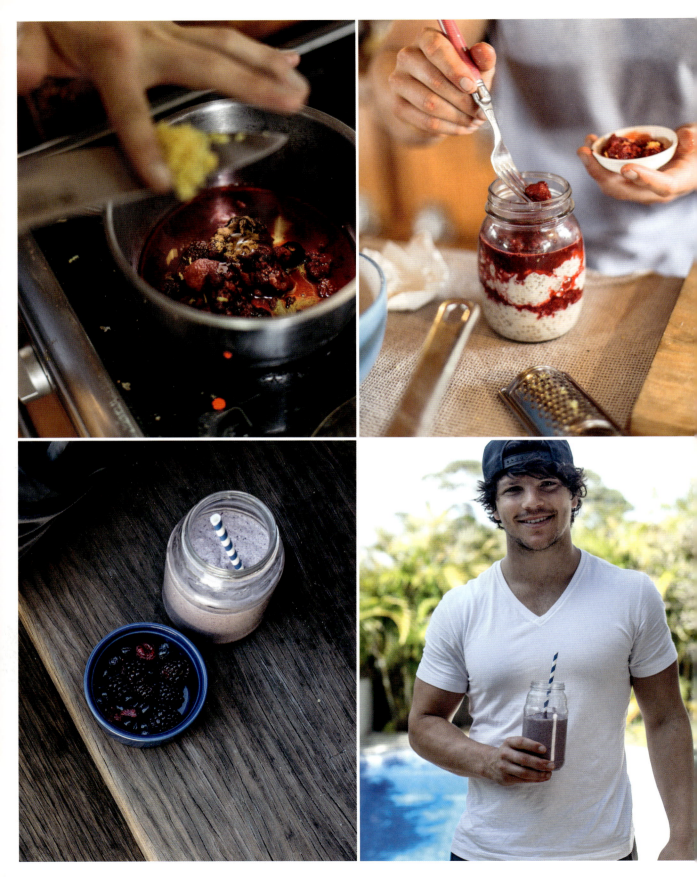

THE HEALTHY COOK

BREAKFAST

BREAKFAST

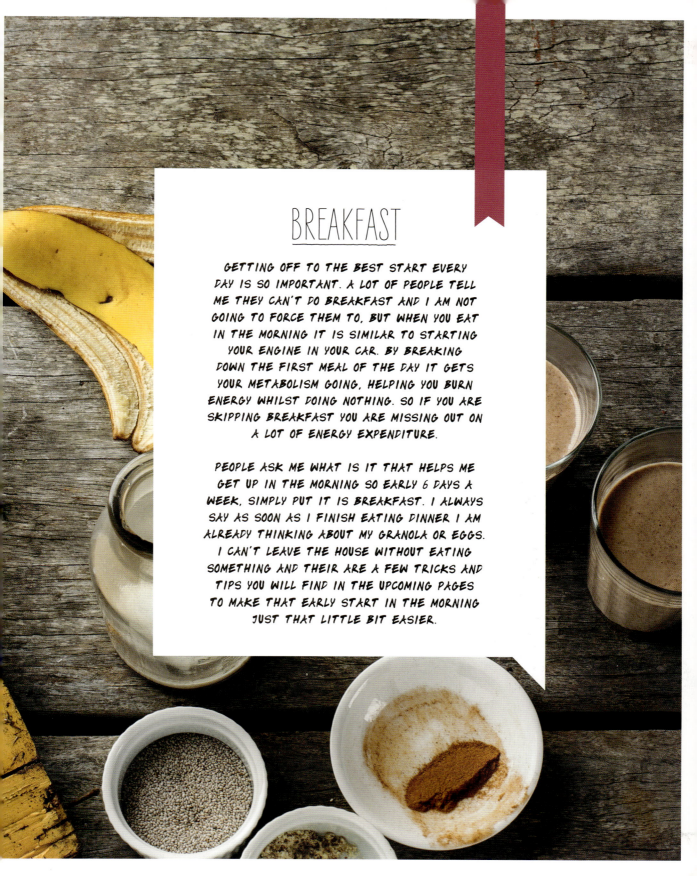

BREAKFAST

Getting off to the best start every day is so important. A lot of people tell me they can't do breakfast and I am not going to force them to, but when you eat in the morning it is similar to starting your engine in your car. By breaking down the first meal of the day it gets your metabolism going, helping you burn energy whilst doing nothing. So if you are skipping breakfast you are missing out on a lot of energy expenditure.

People ask me what is it that helps me get up in the morning so early 6 days a week, simply put it is breakfast. I always say as soon as I finish eating dinner I am already thinking about my granola or eggs. I can't leave the house without eating something and their are a few tricks and tips you will find in the upcoming pages to make that early start in the morning just that little bit easier.

BREAKFAST

BIRCHER WITH ZESTY RASPBERRY SAUCE

ONE OF THE BIGGEST THINGS I LIKE TO ENDORSE IS MAKING MEALS IN BULK, IT SAVES TIME AND YOU HAVE MORE OF THE DELICIOUS TASTING FOODS. THIS IS ONE OF THOSE MEALS THAT IS QUICKER TO PREPARE THAN A CUP OF TEA AS WELL. IT IS PERFECT FOR ME IN THE MORNING WHEN I HAVE AN EARLY SESSION AND NEED TO GET READY IN A HURRY.

INGREDIENTS

- ⅔ cup oats
- 1 ½ cups almond milk, or full cream milk or water
- ½ tbsp chia seeds
- ¼ cup quinoa flakes (optional)
- ¼ cup toasted walnuts

Zesty Raspberry Sauce

- Juice and zest of half a Lemon
- ½ star anise
- ½ tsp ground cinnamon
- 1 tbsp of honey or agave
- ½ vanilla pod with seeds or ½ tsp vanilla extract
- 1 cup of frozen raspberries

METHOD

Combine all ingredients, except the walnuts, in a bowl and place in the fridge overnight.

In the morning, layer with the raspberry sauce and walnuts and enjoy.

Zesty Raspberry Sauce

In a small saucepan, on medium heat, combine all the ingredients. Allow to heat through for 5 minutes (but you want the berries to hold their shape so avoid mixing towards the latter stages).

Once there is a good sauce base, with some well held raspberries (5 - 7 minutes), remove from the heat. Take out the star anise and vanilla pod before serving with your Bircher. It offers a nice warm contrast to the Bircher but the sauce can also be served cold.

You can store this in the fridge and use it as a spread or a healthy dessert sauce as well :)

SNAPSHOT

SERVES: **2**

PROTEIN	FATS	CARBS
8.4g	3.3g (0.5g) saturated	24.7g (7.5g) sugars

per serve

BREAKFAST

CHOC BANANA PROTEIN SHAKE

WHENEVER I FINISH A WORKOUT I WANT TO FEEL LIKE I HAVE EARNED MY SHAKE. EVEN THOUGH I AM IDEALLY BUGGERED, I KNOW HOW IMPORTANT IT IS TO FEED MY BODY FOR RECOVERY. AFTER ALL, YOUR FOOD IS 70% OF YOUR GOAL SET.

INGREDIENTS

- 1 banana
- ¼ cup LSA (Linseed, Sunflower Seed, Almond Meal)
- 1 scoop chocolate protein powder
- 1 cup almond milk
- 2 tsp chia seeds
- 1 tsp ground cinnamon

METHOD

Combine all ingredients in a blender and process until smooth.

Note: It is imperative that you ingest some sort of high protein intake within the first 20 minutes of finishing a workout. This is what scientists like to call your 'glycolytic window". Essentially it is the time where your body is most efficiently working to transport proteins and sugars to the repairing site of muscles. If you miss that window it is worse than missing the post office on a Friday afternoon and you could be sweating for nothing. I have many variations of my post workout shake and more often than not they consist of what I think I could break down in my blender. This one is great for recovery as you get an immediate burst of energy from the banana. However if you are trying to lose weight I would recommend using berries instead of banana as they have less sugar and are a slower releasing carbohydrate.

SNAPSHOT

SERVES: **2**

- TIME
- HEALTHY
- SKILL

PROTEIN	FATS	CARBS
32.6g	3.4g (1.6g) saturated	25.8g (16.2g) sugars

per serve

MY BREAKFAST FRITTATA

I remember the first time I made this dish I just pulled it out of the oven, served it up and went to get my pen and paper to record the measurements and when I came back I found the boys tucking in as if it was a morning pizza. I guess to an extent it is. Obviously a great quick way to serve 5 people breakfast... it's proven.

INGREDIENTS

- 1 brown onion, sliced
- 1 leek, sliced
- 3 rashers bacon/pancetta, sliced (optional)
- 1 garlic clove, finely chopped
- ½ cup field or button mushrooms, sliced
- 2 handfuls baby spinach
- ½ bunch chives, finely chopped
- 8 eggs
- 100ml almond or full cream milk
- 50g Danish feta
- 2 tbsp olive oil

METHOD

Preheat the grill to 180°C.

Meanwhile, in a saucepan on medium heat, drizzle in 1 tbsp oil before caramelising onions for 10 minutes.

Heat remaining 1 tbsp olive oil in a deep ovenproof frypan on medium heat, add the leeks and sweat for 10 minutes until golden, add the pancetta and garlic and continue to cook for a further 2 minutes. Toss in the mushrooms but refrain from stirring so to get a nice golden edge, if need be, agitate the pan by shaking the handle.

Whisk the milk and eggs together with the chives, spread half the spinach and pancetta evenly on top of the mushrooms before pouring over the whisked eggs. Season with salt and allow the base and sides of the egg to be well cooked before adding in the remaining spinach and pancetta on top.

Place pan under the grill for 8 - 10 minutes.

To serve, add some caramelised onions on top of the frittata and sprinkle over the feta and remaining chives.

SNAPSHOT

SERVES: **8**

- TIME
- HEALTHY
- SKILL

PROTEIN	FATS	CARBS
15.9g	10.8g (3.6g) saturated	2.8g (2.6g) sugars

per serve

BREAKFAST SMOOTHIE

THIS IS MY LIQUID BREAKFAST AS IT CONTAINS THE SLOW RELEASE CARBOHYDRATES YOU NEED TO START YOUR DAY. HIGH IN FIBRE FROM THE CHIA SEEDS AND LSA IT WILL AID IN YOUR DIGESTION AND KEEP YOU SATISFIED FOR A NUMBER OF HOURS. I AM KNOWN TO ADD THE OCCASIONAL SCOOP OF PROTEIN POWDER.

INGREDIENTS

- ¼ cup oats
- ½ handful of raw cashews
- ¼ cup frozen berries (acai if you can get them)
- 1 cup almond milk
- 1 tbsp LSA
- 2 tsp chia seeds
- 1 tsp cinnamon
- 2 tsp honey, agave or maple syrup

METHOD

Combine all ingredients in a blender and pulse until well combined. If you want it really chilled you can use ice, but I prefer to keep my berries really frozen so that the flavour is not diluted through the ice.

Note: A great source of dietary fibre, acai berries are regarded as another modern day superfood. Great for the immune system, acai berries contain a high level of the antioxidant flavanoids. Derived from a native palm tree in South America, they play a vital part in eliminating cancer causing free radicals.

SNAPSHOT   MAKES: 2

TIME		
HEALTHY		
SKILL		

PROTEIN	FATS	CARBS
16.8g	9.2g (2.2g) saturated	45.4g (22.0g) sugars

per serve

CORN FRITTERS WITH AVOCADO SALSA

Corn kernals are an amazing natural sweetener. High in many essential vitamins they offer a great burst of flavour once you chew down on them. This is the perfect summer time breakfast, healthy, colourful and naturally balanced

INGREDIENTS

- 1 sweet corn, kernels removed
- 2 eggs
- ½ handful chives, sliced
- Pinch of salt
- 1 cup almond meal
- ⅔ cup almond milk or regular milk
- 2 tbsp olive oil
- 1 spanish onion, roughly chopped
- 1 tomato, roughly chopped
- ½ handful coriander leaves, roughly chopped
- 1 cucumber, roughly chopped
- Juice of ½ lemon
- 2 tbsp of pepitas, pounded in mortar and pestle
- ½ long red chilli, seeds removed, finely chopped
- 1 avocado, diced

METHOD

In a bowl combine the almond meal, onion, eggs, salt, milk and corn

Heat a frypan to high heat and add the oil. Using a spoon, shape the corn mix into 15 patties and apply to the heat. Cook on each side for 2 minutes or until golden brown and cooked through. Remove and set aside on a plate until all fritters are cooked.

In a separate bowl combine Spanish onion, tomato, cucumber, coriander leaves, avocado and chilli.

Just before serving squeeze over some lemon juice and mix through.

To serve stack three fritters on top of each other, sandwiching the avocado salsa in-between and finish with a sprinkle of pepitas. Alternatively you can serve them individually and top a spoonful of the salsa on each.

SNAPSHOT

SERVES: **5**

- TIME
- HEALTHY
- SKILL

PROTEIN	FATS	CARBS
17.0g	11.2g (2.3g) saturated	10.2g (7.2g) sugars

per serve

MY HOMEMADE GRANOLA

I TALK A LOT ABOUT MAKING THINGS IN BULK AT THE START OF THE WEEK. WELL THIS IS MY GO TO. IT OFFERS A GREAT DEPTH OF FLAVOUR AND CAN KEEP FOR AGES. WITH THE ASSORTMENT OF NUTS AND THE ADDITION OF HONEY, IT IS A MUCH BETTER ALTERNATIVE TO THE CONFECTIONARY SUGAR PACKETS YOU WILL FIND AT THE SUPERMARKET. I USE COCONUT OIL AS IT IS GREAT FOR THE HEART, BUT ALSO BECAUSE I LOVE THE NUTTINESS IT PROVIDES.

INGREDIENTS

- ½ cup raw cashews
- ½ cup walnuts
- ½ cup almonds (ideally activated)
- 1 tsp cinnamon
- 3 tbsp honey
- 1 ½ tbsps coconut oil (can also use macadamia or grapeseed)
- 2 cups rolled oats
- ½ cup quinoa flakes (optional)
- ¼ cup desiccated coconut

METHOD

Preheat oven to 160°C.

Combine the nuts in a mortar and pestle and give them a light bashing. You want them to still keep their shape but just be a bit deformed.

In a mixing bowl combine all the ingredients except the desiccated coconut.

Line a baking tray with baking paper and carefully pour mixture out onto tray making sure it is evenly spread. Put in the oven for 10 minutes.

Remove from the oven, spoon over the desiccated coconut and taste to see if you want more honey. Stir before putting back in for a further 10 minutes.

Remove from oven and allow to cool, serve with natural yoghurt and fresh fruit. I love my berries.

SNAPSHOT

SERVES: **4**

- TIME
- HEALTHY
- SKILL

PROTEIN	FATS	CARBS
14.5g	22.1g (4.7g) saturated	47.8g (5.3g) sugars

per serve

BREAKFAST

FRUIT SMOOTHIE

ONE OF THE BEST THINGS WITH HAVING A BLENDER IS YOU CAN PUT ANY COMBINATION TOGETHER THAT SUITS. MY SECRET HERE IS INSTEAD OF USING ICE, WHICH CAN DILUTE THE FLAVOR, I FREEZE THE BANANA AND PURCHASE FROZEN BERRIES. IT IS JUST AS REFRESHING AND TASTES EVEN MORE AMAZING AS IT IS NOT WATERED DOWN.

INGREDIENTS

- ¼ cup frozen berries
- ¼ cup pineapple, I use mango when it is in season
- 2 tbsp desiccated coconut
- 1 cup coconut water
- 1 banana
- 2 tsp chia seeds

METHOD

Put all the ingredients in a blender and process until combined. I try to avoid ice as I believe it dilutes the flavour so I tend to freeze my fruit and that makes it just as cold.

Note: Coconut water is a natural sports drink. Containing electrolytes along with magnesium and potassium it is an ideal beverage to remain hydrated without the inclusion of additional simple sugars. One of coconut water's other key benefits is the positive influence it has on your skin.

SNAPSHOT

SERVES: **2**

- TIME
- HEALTHY
- SKILL

PROTEIN	CARBS	FATS
2.2g	1.1g (0.6g) saturated	20.7g (12.2g) sugars

per serve

BREAKFAST

SWEET POTATO FRITTERS
WITH CHILLI TOMATO JAM, OVEN BAKED MUSHROOMS AND HERB OIL

IF YOU HAVE TIME THESE WILL SURELY IMPRESS YOUR GUESTS. THIS RECIPE IS PAN FRIED BUT IF YOU WANT TO TREAT YOURSELF ADD A LITTLE EXTRA OIL AND GET THEM CRISPIER!

INGREDIENTS

- 1 large sweet potato, grated and drained
- 2 eggs
- 2 tsp ground cumin
- 2 tsp ground coriander
- pinch of salt
- 1 tsp black peppercorns
- 1 tbsp Danish feta
- ¼ cup almond meal (optional)
- 1 onion, finely chopped
- 3 garlic cloves, finely chopped
- 3 tomatoes
- 1 tbsp maple syrup
- Pinch of salt
- ¼ cup white wine vinegar
- 1 cup field mushrooms, sliced
- 1 tbsp olive oil
- Pinch of salt
- 4 sprigs of thyme
- 12 slices of pancetta (optional)

METHOD

Preheat oven to 180°C.

In a bowl combine sweet potato, eggs, cumin, coriander, salt, peppercorns and feta. Pour the mixture into a colander and allow excess moisture to drain out for 15 minutes. If you want to add the almond meal as an extra precaution to hold it together, do so once drained.

For the tomato jam, brown the onion and garlic on high heat in oil for 3 - 4 minutes. Pulse the tomatoes in a blender until juicy, this should only take 10 - 15 seconds, and add to the onions. Stir for one minute before adding the maple syrup, salt and vinegar. Bring to a boil, reduce heat to low and allow to simmer for 10 - 12 minutes to thicken. Set aside before serving.

Line a baking tray with baking paper and spread the mushrooms evenly on top. Sprinkle over garlic, salt and thyme before drizzling with olive oil. Put in the oven for 12 - 15 minutes, or until golden. Set aside for serving.

For the Fritters, shape into an oval using the palm of your hand and a spoon. Add oil to a hot frypan and once smoking add the fritters to get a sizzling sound. Continue to turn them until they are golden all over, this should take no longer than 2 - 3 minutes.

To serve, spoon jam onto the bottom of a plate. Add a layer of mushrooms then pop three fritters around the circle. If using pancetta spread around the plate and top with a few leaves of thyme.

Note: If you feel like you have earned a treat, try the crispy fritters. Add enough grapeseed oil to a small saucepan or wok that will coat half the fritters. To test if the oil is hot enough add a tiny piece of fritter to the oil and if it bubbles away, carefully place a fritter in. Continue to turn to ensure the entire outer surface becomes crispy. Remove onto a paper towel before serving

The nutritional information does not include optional ingredients and is based on the pan fried and not the crispy fritters.

SNAPSHOT

SERVES: **5**

- TIME
- HEALTHY
- SKILL

PROTEIN	FATS	CARBS
9.1g	12.4g (3.4g) saturated	22g (9.6g) sugars

per serve

BREAKFAST

GREEN SMOOTHIE

These are becoming so popular and I love trying out everyone's different recipes. Mine offers a great source of antioxidants and immune fighting benefits.

INGREDIENTS

2 kale leaves and stems

1 knob of ginger

1 cup coconut water

2 tsp chia seeds

1 green apple

½ avocado

METHOD

Combine all the ingredients together in a blender and process until smooth.

Notes: With the inclusion of avocado for the obvious quality fat, it also produces a creamier texture. You can substitute the kale for spinach, or even add both, as always, mix and match. It does help if you have a powerful blender as it will completely break down the leaves and make it really smooth, but its not a necessity.

SNAPSHOT

SERVES: **2**

- TIME
- HEALTHY
- SKILL

PROTEIN	FATS	CARBS
1.4g	6.8g (1.0g) saturated	14g (12.8g) sugars

per serve

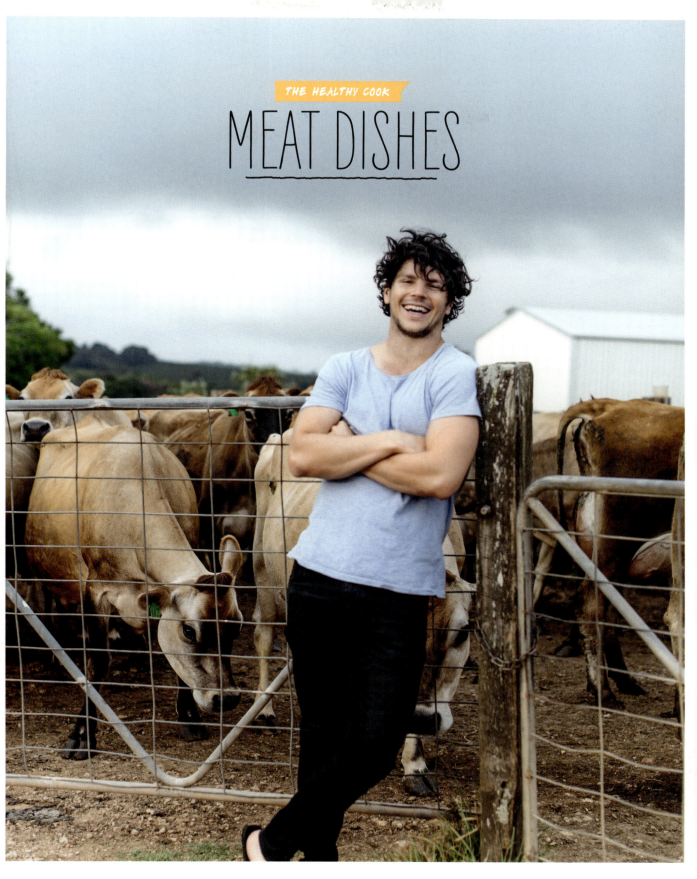

THE HEALTHY COOK
MEAT DISHES

MEAT DISHES

MEAT DISHES

Without a doubt the thing I love to eat most in this world is meat. Fantastic for muscular repair and development, it is something you really should be trying to consume twice per day. Meat is generally the hero of a dish and throughout this chapter I have used a number of different techniques to educate and inspire you to alter the way you cook yours in other cuisines. However, be aware to always balance your meals as meat does contain a number of toxins. Too many toxins can affect the body's cellular structure. Just like chocolate know how much is too much.

MEAT DISHES

SMOKY CHICKEN LEGS

PULL UP A TABLE, GET OUT YOUR SERVING DISH AND TURN THE TELEVISION TO THE SPORT CHANNEL. THESE ARE AS HEALTHY FINGER FOOD AS THEY COME. WITH THE OBVIOUS USE OF SPICES, THE MEAT IS OVEN BAKED AND NOT DEEP FRIED, MEANING LESS SATURATED FAT AND A GREAT WAY TO ENJOY THE GAME. JUST DON'T GET CAUGHT UP IN THE FOOD TOO MUCH, OTHERWISE YOU WONT GET THE SCORE.

INGREDIENTS

8 chicken legs (drumstick & thigh)

2 tbsp cup olive oil

Spice Mix

1 tbsp paprika, smoked if possible

2 tsp cayenne pepper

2 tsp ground cinnamon

1 tbsp cumin, ground

2 good pinches salt

2 tsp black pepper, ground

METHOD

Combine spice mix in a bowl.

Cut 4 slices into the chicken about ½ cm deep, this will allow spice mix to penetrate flesh, enhance the flavour and cook the chicken quicker.

Place chicken in a mixing bowl. Evenly pour over the spice mix and rub it in with your hands ensuring it gets into the sliced section of the meat. Cover with plastic wrap and allow to marinade in the fridge for at least 30 minutes, but the longer the better.

Preheat the oven to 180°C.

Line a baking tray with baking paper and place the chicken evenly on top. Sprinkle with a final seasoning of salt... from a height of course, and place in the oven for 15 - 20 minutes. As it is leg meat it will naturally be pinker than breast but of course you don't want it raw.

SNAPSHOT

SERVES: **4**

TIME
HEALTHY
SKILL

PROTEIN	FATS	CARBS
25.5g	14.5g (3.0g) saturated	6.2g (2.6g) sugars

per serve

MEAT DISHES

PULL APART LAMB
WITH ROASTED BUTTER BEANS

IT'S HARD TO CONVEY A SENSE OF SMELL THROUGH WORDS, BUT IF YOU ARE COOKING THIS DISH, THE AROMA THAT ENVELOPES THE HOUSE IS UNBELIEVABLE. HIGH IN PROTEIN FROM THE LAMB AND BEANS, ITS A GREAT ALTERNATIVE TO USE FOR TORTILLAS.

INGREDIENTS

- 2 tbsp extra virgin olive oil
- 1 leg of lamb
- 6 cloves of garlic
- 3 sprigs of rosemary
- 2 onions, sliced
- ½ a leek, thinly sliced
- 4 cans of butter beans
- 1 bunch of fresh thyme
- 1 bay leaf
- ½ bunch of fresh coriander
- ½ bunch of fresh flat leaf parsley
- 250ml chicken stock
- Salt & pepper

METHOD

Preheat the oven to 140°C.

Slice up three garlic cloves, stab the lamb leg a number of times with a sharp blade and stuff the holes with the garlic and rosemary leaves. Drizzle with a good amount of olive oil, sprinkle with salt and pepper and place on a rack in the top section of the oven. Place a roasting tray below the rack allowing all the juice to be caught. Cook for 6 - 8 hours or until lamb pulls away from the bone. Cover and set aside.

With an hour left for the lamb to cook, add one tablespoon of oil to a frypan on high heat.

Brown the leek, onion and three remaining garlic cloves in 1 tbsp of oil. Meanwhile tie the thyme, coriander, bay leaf and parsley together and set aside.

Once the onion mixture is golden brown add the butter beans, bury the tied bunch of herbs and pour in the chicken stock. Season with salt and pepper and, if you feel like you have earned it, add in the reserved lamb juices (otherwise place in a clean roasting tray) and cook for 30 - 40 minutes or until liquid is absorbed.

Remove the herb bunch and serve the beans with the pulled apart lamb.

SNAPSHOT   SERVES: 6

TIME
HEALTHY
SKILL

PROTEIN	FATS	CARBS
39g	15.5g (4.8g) saturated	15.0g (4.4g) sugars

per serve

MEAT DISHES

EYE FILLET STEAK
WITH SALSA VERDE & OVEN ROASTED SWEET TOMATOES

COOKING THE PERFECT STEAK IS AN ART AND EVERY GREAT BBQ'ER HAS THEIR SPECIAL METHOD. AFTER BEING FORTUNATE TO MEET AND HANG OUT WITH THE GREAT HESTON BLUMENTHAL I COULDN'T NOT GO PAST HIS METHOD OF TURNING THE MEAT EVERY 15 SECONDS. HIS REASONING WAS PURELY SCIENTIFIC AND NATURALLY I AM NOT GOING TRY AND EDUCATE YOU, RATHER THAN TO SAY HE IS TOO SMART TO NOT TRUST.

INGREDIENTS

- 4 eye fillet steaks
- 1 garlic clove, roughly chopped
- 1 bunch thyme
- 2 sprigs rosemary
- 1 tsp salt
- 1 punnet of cherry tomatoes, halved
- 2 tsp honey
- Olive oil

Salsa Verde

- 1 handful of basil, roughly chopped
- 1 tbsp capers
- 5 gherkins, roughly chopped
- 5 anchovies
- ½ handful mint
- 100ml olive oil
- Juice and zest of ½ lemon
- ½ tsp salt

METHOD

Preheat oven to 180°C.

Sprinkle a pinch of salt on each side of the steaks and allow to sit aside for 15 minutes. This will help it get a nice crust.

In a mortar and pestle add the garlic and rosemary and pound to a nice paste. Add a little oil to assist. Tie the bunch of thyme together and place with the leaf end facing down. Pound to release some of the leaves but still keep the stems to make a brush.

Remove the thyme brush and set aside before adding 2 tbsp of oil and mixing, set aside.

Line a baking tray with baking paper and spread tomatoes on top, drizzle with honey, sprinkle with salt and pop in the oven for 8 - 12 minutes or until nice and shrivelled.

Meanwhile, using a stick blender, processor or blender, add all the ingredients for the salsa verde apart from the oil. Turn the machine on and gradually add the oil. Season with lemon juice and salt to taste.

Put a griddle pan on to high heat. Dip the thyme brush in the herb oil and gently brush both sides of the steaks before adding them to the griddle pan. The pan must be really hot and you should hear a nice sizzle as the meat touches the pan.

To cook the steak, turn it every 15 seconds and every single time you flip it over, baste it in the oil using the thyme brush. When you flip the steaks try to align the griddle marks with the previous ones already made.

To get nice criss-cross griddle marks, after 60 - 75 seconds turn the meat 90 degrees to cook for another 60 seconds. Turn over and repeat the process before resting under foil for 5 minutes.

Serve with tomatoes and a dollop of salsa verde.

SNAPSHOT

SERVES: **4**

- TIME
- HEALTHY
- SKILL

PROTEIN	FATS	CARBS
35.8g	26.2g (5.3g) saturated	7.9g (5.2g) sugars

per serve

STEP BY STEP
EYE FILLET STEAK WITH SALSA VERDE

MEAT DISHES

GREEN MASALA

The first time I tried making this was in the house with other contestants, my other family. I am not sure if it still stands, but it was claimed to be the greatest curry they had tasted. I am not sure what Rishi thought about that.

INGREDIENTS

- 1 onion, roughly chopped
- 2 green chillies, soaked in water for 15 mins, seeded and finely chopped
- 1 handful of fresh coriander, roughly chopped
- 1 handful of mint, roughly chopped
- ½ cup cashews, soaked in water for 15 minutes
- 1 knob of ginger, finely chopped
- 2 cloves of garlic finely chopped
- 1kg chicken, skin removed and cut into pieces or 600g chicken drumsticks
- 200g natural yoghurt
- Juice of a lemon
- 1 tbsp garam masala
- 1 tbsp cumin seeds
- 1 tbsp coriander seeds
- 1 cup chicken stock
- 150ml coconut milk
- 1 tsp palm sugar (optional)
- 1 tsp salt
- 1 tbsp fish sauce
- 1 cup of brown long grain rice
- 2 cups of water

Garam Masala

- 1 tsp cloves
- 1 tbsp cardamon pods
- ½ cinnamon stick
- 1 tbsp black peppercorns

METHOD

Heat oil in a large frypan on high heat and brown the onions.

In a mortar and pestle or food processor pound the cashews, coriander, mint and chilli. Add the onions and pound to a paste consistency.

Add the paste along with the ginger, garlic and chicken to the yoghurt and mix until well combined. Add the juice of half a lemon then cover and put in the fridge for at least 30 minutes, ideally 2 hours.

If you are using whole seeds for the garam masala, dry roast them along with the coriander and cumin seeds in a little frypan for 1 minute or until fragrant, this will enhance the flavour they bring to the dish. Then pound to a powder in a mortar and pestle or spice grinder.

Add the coconut oil to a deep frypan on high heat and once it has melted add the mustard seeds and fry for 20 seconds.

Next, add the entire yoghurt mix. Once chicken is brown, or seared, add the garam masala along with coriander and cumin and mix through for 5 minutes.

Deglaze the pan with the chicken stock and add in the coconut milk. Cover with a lid and turn the heat to low to simmer for at least 45 minutes, stirring every so often.

Whilst the sauce is simmering, put the rice in a saucepan with the water and cover with a lid on high heat. Bring to a boil and allow to simmer 12 minutes or until water is evaporated and rice has cooked through. Remove from heat.

Remove the lid and start to balance the flavours with fish sauce, salt, palm sugar and remaining juice from the lemon. Use my measurements, however also taste to see if you like them, you may want it a little sweeter or more acidic.

Keep the lid off and allow mix to thicken for another 10 minutes, serve immediately with brown rice.

SNAPSHOT   SERVES: 5

TIME		
HEALTHY		
SKILL		

PROTEIN	FATS	CARBS
29.2g	17.8g (8.9g) saturated	30.7g (8.2g) sugars

per serve

MEAT DISHES

BUTTERFLIED LAMB
IN A MIDDLE EASTERN RUB

IF YOU DON'T KNOW HOW TO BUTTERFLY A LAMB GET YOUR BUTCHER TO DO IT FOR YOU. IT'S A QUICK WAY TO COOK YOUR MEAT WITH MINIMAL EFFORT. I LOVE THE COLOUR AND ZESTY FLAVOUR YOU GET FROM THE SUMAC. MAKE IT FOR A PICNIC OR MID WEEK DINNER. ITS PERFECT FOR LEFTOVERS FOR SALADS AND WRAPS THE FOLLOWING FEW DAYS.

INGREDIENTS

- 1 leg of lamb, butterflied
- 1 tbsp salt
- 2 tbsp black peppercorns
- 1 tbsp coriander seeds
- 2 tsp sumac
- 1 tbsp cumin seeds
- 2 garlic cloves, finely chopped
- Onion powder (optional)
- Juice and zest of a whole lemon
- 1/3 cup olive oil

METHOD

In a small frypan, on high heat, dry roast the peppercorns, cumin and coriander seeds for 1 minute.

Grind to a rough powder in a mortar and pestle. Add the sumac, lemon zest, salt, garlic and onion powder (if using) and stir through to combine.

Add to a mixing bowl with the oil.

Place the lamb, spread out, in a marinading tray and pour over the contents from the mixing bowl. Using your hands, spread the spices around both sides of the meat before covering with cling film and allowing to marinade in the fridge for 30 minutes to 2 hours.

Preheat BBQ to high heat.

Remove the lamb from the fridge, squeeze the lemon juice over the top, sprinkle the skin with a little more salt before placing flesh side down on the grill, cover and cook for 7 minutes.

Turn meat over onto the skin side and again cover and cook for 10 - 12 minutes before finishing back on the flesh side for a further 2 - 3 minutes with the lid off.

Remove from BBQ and cover with foil to rest for 7 - 10 minutes.

Slice and serve with a lovely cauliflower roasted salad.

SNAPSHOT

SERVES: **6**

- TIME
- HEALTHY
- SKILL

PROTEIN	FATS	CARBS
38.2g	16.7g (5.2g) saturated	3.7g (0.8g) sugars

per serve

MEAT DISHES

CHICKEN PARMY

JUST LIKE ANYONE, I LOVE A GOOD CHICKEN PARMY. ORIGINATING IN ITALY IT HAS BECOME A STAPLE ON EVERY PUB MENU. IT BECAME A MISSION OF MINE TO REMAKE THIS DISH IN ORDER TO SATISFY MY MATES APPETITES. MORE OFTEN THAN NOT I DON'T LIKE TO EAT WHAT GOES THROUGH THEIR MIND. SO IN ORDER TO HAVE A SIT DOWN MEAL WITH THEM I HAD TO COME UP A MIDDLE GROUND. I HAVE DEFINITELY FOUND IT.

INGREDIENTS

- 4 chicken breasts, skinless
- ¼ cup pepitas, crushed
- 2 tbsp sesame seeds
- ½ cup almond meal
- 1 tsp salt
- 2 tbsp olive oil
- 1 onion, finely chopped
- 1 garlic clove, finely chopped
- 1 tbsp tomato paste
- ½ handful fresh basil, finely chopped
- 1 tsp fennel seeds
- 3 tomatoes, diced
- ¼ cup red wine vinegar
- 100 grams ricotta, drained

METHOD

Preheat your grill to medium heat.

Sandwich each breast between 2 sheets of glad wrap, then using a mallet or a bottle of wine if its closer ;) bash the chicken to ½ to 1cm thick. Repeat with each breast.

In a mixing bowl combine the almond meal, salt, sesame seeds and crushed pepitas. Pour onto a plate.

Coat each side of chicken breast in the almond meal mix. Transfer to a clean plate and repeat for each chicken portion and set aside or in the fridge.

Brown onion and garlic and add tomatoes. Cook through for 6 minutes.

Add the tomato paste, basil, fennel seeds and red wine vinegar. Turn the heat to low and simmer for 15 minutes with lid off to reduce and thicken.

In a separate frypan add the olive oil on high heat. Add the chicken to the pan and cook for 1 minute on each side or until golden. Transfer to a lined baking tray, top with 2 tablespoons of the tomato sauce and then finish with 1 spoonful of ricotta before putting under the grill for a final minute.

Serve with the Italian quinoa salad or the good old fashioned sweet potato chips.

SNAPSHOT

SERVES: **4**

TIME
HEALTHY
SKILL

PROTEIN	FATS	CARBS
37.8g	21.3g (3.7g) saturated	4.8g (3.7g) sugars

per serve

MEAT DISHES

LAMB CUTLETS WITH MACADAMIA CRUST

Mum loves serving up cutlets, except she usually makes a jam spread to coat. Growing up I was always searching for a little more crunch in my foods, hence the predominant involvement of nuts. Taking the inspiration of a dukkah crumb I found this method a delicious way to meet my cravings.

INGREDIENTS

- ¼ cup macadamia nuts
- ¼ cup hazelnuts
- 1 tbsp coriander seeds
- 1 tbsp cumin seeds
- 1 tsp salt
- 2 tsp fennel seeds
- 1 rack of lamb
- 2 tsp olive oil

Middle Eastern Carrots

- 1 tbsp coriander seeds
- 1 tbsp cumin seeds
- 2 tsp sumac
- 2 tsp black peppercorns, ground
- 1 garlic clove, finely chopped
- 2 tbsp cider vinegar
- 1 tbsp olive oil
- 1 large bunch of dutch carrots

Mint Yoghurt

- ½ cup natural yoghurt
- ½ handful of fresh mint, finely shredded
- Zest of ½ a Lemon

SNAPSHOT

SERVES: 4

- TIME
- HEALTHY
- SKILL

PROTEIN	FATS	CARBS
29.7g	28.6g (4.8g) saturated	5.6g (4.8g) sugars

per serve

METHOD

Preheat oven to 200°C.

Line a baking tray and spread hazelnuts on top. Place in the oven for 5 - 7 minutes or until skin easily peels away.

Remove nuts from the oven and place within a tea towel to remove skin. Rub the tea towel with your hands for 30 seconds before using your fingers to peel back any extras that are being tricky. Allow to cool.

Dry roast the coriander, fennel and cumin seeds for 1 minute before roughly pounding in a mortar and pestle (ideally you want them to still hold their shape for texture). Remove to another bowl.

Place the skinless hazelnuts into a mortar and pestle along with the macadamias and grind until they reach the size of the seeds.

Combine the seeds and nuts along with the salt before spreading out onto a lined baking tray.

Rub the oil over the outer side of the lamb then carefully dip the oil side in the nut crust mix. Roll the lamb to get as much of the mix onto the flesh as possible.

Sit the lamb upright on top of the mound of crust, set aside.

For the carrots, combine the seeds, garlic, peppercorns and sumac in a bowl.

Toss carrots in cider vinegar and oil, then coat in half the mix.

Place the lamb on the top rack and the carrots on the bottom. Cook the lamb for 20 minutes, before removing to cover with foil to rest. At this point remove the carrots as well and coat with the rest of the mix before putting back in the oven for a further 10 minutes.

Combine elements of mint yoghurt in a bowl, set aside.

To serve, portion out carrots, slice up lamb and serve with mint yoghurt.

STEP BY STEP GUIDE ▶

STEP BY STEP
LAMB CUTLETS WITH MACADAMIA CRUST

MEAT DISHES

MUSTARD AND PEPPERCORN ROO
WITH BRAISED LENTILS

I REGARD KANGAROO AS A PROTEIN SUPERFOOD. IT IS RIDICULOUSLY LOW IN FAT PURELY BECAUSE THE ANIMAL ITSELF IS VERY ACTIVE. PEOPLE OFTEN GET PUT OFF BY THE FACT IT IS UNUSUAL TO EAT SOMETHING THAT IS NOT REALLY FARMED. ITS BEAUTIFUL, BUT HAS A TENDENCY TO BE CHEWY DUE TO ITS MINIMAL FAT. SO AVOID OVERCOOKING IT AND IT WILL STILL BE BEAUTIFUL.

INGREDIENTS

- 1 red capsicum
- 600g kangaroo steaks
- ½ head broccoli
- 1 onion, finely chopped
- 2 garlic cloves, finely chopped
- 2 carrots, sliced
- 1 leek, sliced
- 1 cup lentils
- 2 ½ cups chicken stock
- 3 sprigs thyme
- ¼ cup white wine vinegar
- ½ handful parsley, finely chopped
- 1 tsp salt

Mustard marinade

- 1 tbsp whole black peppercorns
- 2 tbsp Dijon mustard
- Juice of ½ lemon

METHOD

If you have a gas top, using your tongs carefully roast the capsicum on all sides until skin is all dark and wrinkly or, preheat your oven to 200°C, place the capsicum on a lined tray and place in the oven for 15 - 20 minutes or until all skin is shrivelled and wrinkly. Place the capsicum in a bowl and cover with cling wrap for 10 minutes so that skin will peel away easily. Turn oven to 180°C.

Combine kangaroo with the mustard marinade, cover and set aside.

Steam or boil broccoli heads for 1 - 2 minutes, or until soft.

Add oil to a hot pan, add onion, garlic, carrot and leeks and soften. Purée the broccoli with a little oil and add to vegetables.

Next add lentils, thyme, stock and vinegar and cover with a lid, turn to low and simmer for 30 minutes, or until lentils are soft.

Add salt and fold in parsley and capsicum before setting aside.

In a griddle pan, on high heat, sear the steaks on either side for 1 - 2 minutes, to get a nice colour, before putting in the oven for 3 - 4 minutes.

Remove from oven and cover with foil to rest for 5 minutes.

Slice the steak and serve with lentils.

SNAPSHOT

SERVES: **5**

TIME
HEALTHY
SKILL

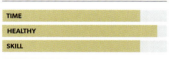

PROTEIN	FATS	CARBS
36.7g	2.4g (0.5g) saturated	12.4g (3.1g) sugars

per serve

MEAT DISHES

COUNTRY CHICKEN
SWEET POTATO TOP PIE

THERE IS NOTHING BETTER THAN WATCHING MUM OR DAD PULL THAT GREAT SMELLING PIE OUT OF THE OVEN ON A COLD WINTER NIGHT. BY AVOIDING THE PASTRY YOU DON'T GET THAT HUGE INTAKE OF SATURATED FAT. ON TOP OF THIS THERE ARE A NUMBER OF GREAT VEGETABLES INSIDE AND A GREAT SUBSTANCE OF CARBOHYDRATE IN THE SWEET POTATO, BUT I COULDN'T AVOID A FAMILY FAVOURITE.

INGREDIENTS

- 1kg chicken deboned or 600g chicken drumsticks
- 2 tsp salt
- 2 tbsp oil
- 1 onion, finely chopped
- 2 garlic cloves, finely chopped
- 1 carrot, sliced
- 1 celery, sliced
- 1 leek, sliced
- 1 cup chicken stock
- 2 tbsp white wine vinegar
- 2 tsp black pepper, ground
- 3 sprigs thyme
- 2 sprigs rosemary
- 1 bay leaf
- 2 medium sweet potatoes, peeled and cubed evenly
- ¼ cup almond milk

METHOD

Preheat oven to 180°C.

Line a baking tray with baking paper. Place chicken on top then sprinkle with one teaspoon of salt and drizzle over one tablespoon of oil and cook in the oven for 12 - 15 minutes, or until tender.

Remove from oven, discard skin and allow to cool for 5 minutes. Using two forks, shred the meat making sure it is still chunky, set aside.

Add the remaining oil to a medium saucepan on high heat. Brown the onion and garlic before adding the carrots, celery and leek.

Once browned add the chicken, stir for one minute before deglazing with the stock.

Next add the white wine vinegar, pepper, thyme, rosemary, bay leaf and remaining salt. Turn the heat to low, cover and allow to simmer for 30 - 40 minutes or until stock has reduced.

Meanwhile, in another saucepan, add the sweet potato and cover with water. Bring to a boil on high heat, before turning to medium heat and allowing to cook for a further 6 - 8 minutes, or until a knife pierces flesh easily.

Drain sweet potato and allow to dry out for two minutes before putting in a blender with the almond milk and processing until smooth. Remove and set aside.

Preheat the grill to medium/high.

Spoon the chicken mix into an ovenproof dish. Spoon the sweet potato mix on top and spread around evenly to get it smooth. Place under the grill for 5 minutes or until the top changes colour.

SNAPSHOT

SERVES: **5**

- TIME
- HEALTHY
- SKILL

PROTEIN	FATS	CARBS
26.6g	7.6g (1.7g) saturated	13.7g (6.3g) sugars

per serve

MEAT DISHES

JUICY CHICKEN BREAST
WITH ROAST PUMPKIN, QUINOA & SPINACH SALAD

I HEAR A LOT ABOUT HOW PEOPLE MUCH PREFER THIGH MEAT OVER BREAST AS IT DOESN'T DRY OUT AND IS NOT CHEWY. UNDERSTANDABLY THIS CAN BE TRUE AS IT CONTAINS A HIGHER LEVEL OF FAT. HOWEVER I WANTED TO SHOW HOW YOU CAN STILL GET THAT TENDER PIECE OF CHICKEN BREAST THAT DOESN'T CLOG YOUR ARTERIES AND.. IN MY OPINION, TASTES MUCH BETTER.

INGREDIENTS

4 chicken breasts, skin on

½ butternut pumpkin, peeled and diced into 2cm cubes

4 good handfuls of baby spinach

1 cup quinoa

Pinch of salt

Honey mustard dressing

1 tbsp honey

1 tbsp whole grain mustard

100ml olive oil

Juice of ½ lemon

METHOD

Preheat the oven to 180°C.

In a mixing bowl add the pumpkin along with a pinch of salt and a drizzle of olive oil and mix through.

Line a baking tray with baking paper and spread the pumpkin on top before putting in the oven for 20 minutes or until coloured and soft to the touch.

In a small saucepan add the quinoa plus 1 ¾ cups of water. Bring to the boil before turning to low and simmering for 12 minutes.

Add oil to a frypan on high heat. Add the chicken skin side down, it should sizzle. This is where practice comes in as you don't want to burn the skin too quickly before the heat penetrates the flesh, so monitor it and if need be, turn the heat down slightly. Once the chicken begins to cook halfway up the sides flip it over, the skin should have a lovely golden colour, and if you have an oven proof frypan place it straight in the oven, if not you can use a roasting or baking tray. Cook for about 5 minutes, or until chicken is springy to the touch. Remove from oven and allow to rest for 5 minutes before slicing.

For the honey mustard dressing, combine all ingredients in a bowl or jar and mix or shake until combined, set aside for serving.

For the salad, turn the saucepan full of quinoa upside down over a mixing bowl and tap it out, because you are not stirring this will prevent the quinoa from going stodgy. Add the spinach and gently toss through the pumpkin, you don't want to break it up.

To serve, spoon onto four plates and top with a sliced chicken breast before drizzling around the honey mustard, being sure not to drizzle over the skin of the chicken so it maintains its crunch.

SNAPSHOT

SERVES: **4**

- TIME
- HEALTHY
- SKILL

PROTEIN	FATS	CARBS
34.4g	19.1g (3.3g) saturated	15.7g (9.0g) sugars

per serve

MEAT DISHES

BEEF TORTILLAS WITH KALE SLAW

ONE OF MY FAVOURITE MEALS TO DISH OUT. MEXICAN IS BECOMING SO POPULAR AND THERE ARE SO MANY DIFFERENT WAYS TO SERVE THIS. YOU WILL SEE A LOT OF MY VARIATIONS OF THESE AT MY POP-UPS BECAUSE THEY ARE FUN AND A JOY TO EAT.

INGREDIENTS

- 1kg beef chuck steak, excess sinew removed & cubed
- ¼ cup buckwheat flour
- 2 tbsp olive or grapeseed oil
- 2 onions, finely chopped
- 2 garlic cloves, finely chopped
- 375ml beef stock
- 4 tomatoes, blitzed in a blender or 1 tin of chopped tomatoes
- 1 tbsp tomato paste (optional)
- 2 tsp chilli powder
- 1 tbsp smoked paprika
- 1 tsp black pepper, ground
- 2 tsp fennel seeds
- 1 tbsp cumin, ground
- 1 tbsp coriander, ground
- 1 tsp salt
- 2 sprigs of rosemary
- 2 bay Leaves
- 12 corn tortillas or tostadas (see page 84)

Kale Slaw

- 1 cup red cabbage, shredded
- 1 cup white cabbage, shredded
- 1 cup kale, stalk removed and shredded
- ¾ cup mayonnaise (see page 22)
- 1 long red chilli, deseeded and finely chopped
- 1 tbsp lemon juice
- 2 tsp paprika

METHOD

Preheat oven to 140°C.

Dust the beef in the flour before shaking off excess and setting aside onto a plate.

Add one tablespoon of oil to a large oven proof pot on high heat on the stove. Add the beef and allow to brown on all sides. It will stick to the bottom, just continue to scrape with a wooden spoon as this will add to the great flavour. Once brown remove the beef and set aside before adding the rest of the oil to the pot and browning the onion and garlic.

Return the beef to the pot and add the stock, tomatoes, paste and spices. Give it a stir for two minutes before burying the rosemary and bay leaves and mixing in the red wine vinegar.

Cover and put in the oven to cook for 6 - 8 hours, or until meat falls apart with a fork. Remove from the oven and allow to cool for 30 minutes with the lid on. Remove meat from pot with tongs, reserving the sauce. Using two forks shred the meat until it is stringy, set aside.

For the slaw, simply combine the cabbages and kale in a bowl. Mix the mayonnaise with the chilli, lemon juice and paprika before adding to the bowl to combine with the leaves. Set aside.

Just before serving, heat a frypan on high heat and dry roast, without oil, the shredded meat for 1 - 2 minutes until crispy (make sure you don't overcrowd the pan). Remove to a plate.

To serve, spoon the beef sauce onto tortillas, stack on some slaw and finish with the crispy beef.

SNAPSHOT   SERVES: 6

- TIME
- HEALTHY
- SKILL

PROTEIN	FATS	CARBS
28.8g	18.6g (9.2g) saturated	27.7g (6.5g) sugars

per serve

STEP BY STEP GUIDE ▶

STEP BY STEP
BEEF TORTILLAS WITH KALE SLAW

MEAT DISHES

SESAME SATAY SKEWERS

PEANUT BUTTER WOULD HAVE TO BE ONE OF MY VICES GROWING UP SO I COULDN'T NOT PUT IN ONE HEALTHY DISH THAT INCORPORATES IT. WITH THE COMBINATION OF COCONUT MILK AND ORGANIC PEANUT BUTTER, THIS DISH HAS AN AMAZING AMOUNT OF QUALITY FAT. BECAUSE WE ARE USING MAPLE SYRUP OUR BODY IS CONSUMING A LESS REFINED FORM OF SUGAR AS WELL.

INGREDIENTS

- 800g chicken thighs, skinless, divided into 2 lengthways
- 2 tbsp lemon juice
- Pinch of salt
- 300ml coconut milk
- 1 long red chilli, seeds removed
- 1 tbsp honey
- 1 tsp garlic, finely chopped
- 1 onion, finely chopped
- 1 tsp soy sauce
- 100g organic, crunchy, peanut butter
- Lemongrass sticks or wooden skewers
- 2 tsp sesame oil
- 2 tsp sesame seeds

METHOD

Combine lemon juice, salt, coconut milk, chilli and chicken in a bowl. Allow to marinade for 30 minutes to 2 hours.

Drain chicken and keep marinade.

In a frypan, on high heat, brown the onion and garlic before adding the reserved marinade. Stir for one minute before adding the honey, soy sauce and peanut butter. Constantly stir to break up the peanut butter then turn heat to low and cook for 10 minutes to slightly thicken.

Pierce the chicken with the wooden skewers or a knife if using lemongrass.

Add the sesame oil to a hot griddle and grill the chicken for two minutes on each side.

Place on a platter and pour over peanut sauce and sprinkle with sesame seeds to finish.

SNAPSHOT

SERVES: **4**

- TIME
- HEALTHY
- SKILL

PROTEIN	FATS	CARBS
22.5g	22.8g (11.6g) saturated	6.7g (5.9g) sugars

per serve

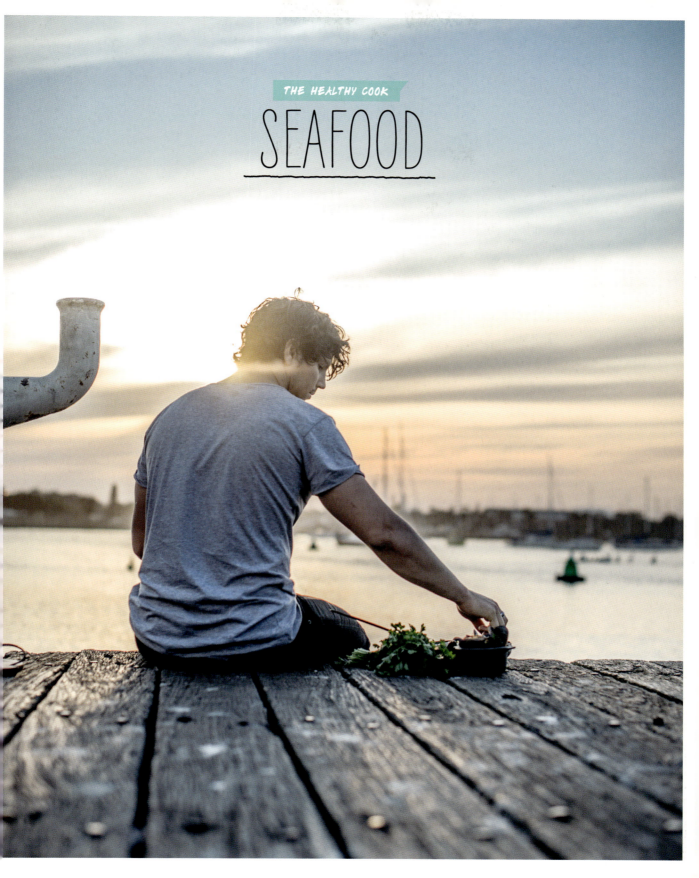

SEAFOOD

SEAFOOD

POACHED SALMON
IN A WALNUT APPLE SALAD WITH HONEY MUSTARD

THE TEXTURE OF A WELL COOKED STEAMED SALMON IS UNBELIEVABLE. TO ME IT'S LIKE BUTTER MELTING IN YOUR MOUTH, JUST WITH MORE PROTEIN, IRON, QUALITY FATS AND LESS YELLOW. ONCE YOU NAIL THIS COOKING METHOD, TRY TO USE IT FOR OTHER DISHES LIKE BREAKFAST WITH POACHED EGGS AND A LOVELY VINAIGRETTE.

INGREDIENTS

- 2 salmon fillets
- 1 cup fish stock (page 26)
- 2 lemongrass stalks, bashed to release flavour
- 2 tsp fennel seeds
- 1 fennel bulb
- 1 Lebanese cucumber, shredded lengthways using a peeler
- ½ cup walnuts
- 1 green apple, cored, halved and thinly sliced
- ½ handful parsley, finely chopped

Honey Mustard Dressing

- 1 tbsp wholegrain mustard
- Juice of ½ lemon
- 1 tbsp honey
- ⅓ cup grapeseed or olive oil (you want one with minimal flavour)

METHOD

Line a steamer with baking paper and cut holes to allow steam to penetrate. Put the salmon on top of the baking paper and set aside.

In a saucepan add the fish stock, fennel seeds and lemon grass. Bring to a boil then turn heat to low. Place steamer on top and cover with a lid. Cook for 8 - 10 minutes or until salmon pulls away nicely to reveal a slight pink flesh.

Meanwhile, combine your cucumber, toasted walnut, apple and parsley in a bowl.

If you have a glass jar add the honey mustard ingredients and shake to combine, if you don't, just mix in a bowl.

Combine half the dressing with the salad mix and toss before transferring to a serving dish.

Remove salmon from steamer, store the steaming juices for a stock, and allow the fish to rest for 3 minutes before flaking off from skin and place on top of salad. If the remaining dressing has been sitting for a while, give it another shake or stir before drizzling over the top to serve.

SNAPSHOT

SERVES: **2**

TIME
HEALTHY
SKILL

PROTEIN	CARBS	FATS
22.5g	22.8g (11.6g) saturated	6.7g (5.9g) sugars

per serve

SEAFOOD

CRISPY SKIN SALMON
AND THREE GRAIN SALAD

Although it looks like a restaurant dish it is actually quite simple. The hardest thing is having enough pots. One of the best things about the dish is the burst of flavour from the pomegranate seeds.

INGREDIENTS

- 4 salmon fillets
- ¾ cup barley
- ¾ cup buckwheat
- ¾ cup quinoa
- Seeds of ½ a pomegranate
- ½ cup slithered almonds
- 1 lemongrass stalk, finely sliced
- ¼ cup cranberries
- 1 tbsp Dijon mustard
- 2 tbsp pomegranate juice
- 2 egg yolks
- Salt
- 1 tbsp of lemon juice
- 125ml grapeseed or pure olive oil

METHOD

Preheat oven to 180°C.

Remove the skin of the salmon by placing the fillet skin side down, carefully cutting into the line where the flesh meets the skin. Grab the skin and move the fillet back and forward against the blade keeping the knife steady until it goes all the way through.

Line a baking tray with baking paper. Sprinkle both sides of the skin with salt and drizzle a little oil before putting another sheet of baking paper on top and sandwiching with another baking tray. Place a weight on top (I use a mortar) and put In the oven for 20 minutes. Remove top layer and allow to dry out. Before serving.

In three separate saucepans add the barley, quinoa and buckwheat. To each of them add a third of lemongrass and 1 ½ cups of water. Bring to the boil before turning to low and simmering for 12 minutes. The barley may take an extra 5 - 10 minutes. Once cooked discard lemongrass stalk.

In a small processor, or using a whisk, combine the mustard, yolk, pomegranate juice and salt. With the motor still running, or whilst still whisking, gradually add a tiny amount of oil. Repeat this step four times, gradually adding more of the oil until there is nothing left and the mix hangs from the whisk or a spoon. Fold through lemon juice to finish.

In a big bowl combine the 3 grains, slithered almonds, pomegranate seeds and cranberries. Set aside before serving.

Heat an oven proof frypan on medium to high heat. Add the oil followed by the fish. You should hear a gentle sizzle. Cook for 2 minutes or until fish turns opaque up the sides before turning over and putting in the oven for 90 seconds, or until the blade comes out warm once inserted into the thickest part of the fish.

To serve, place a few spoonfuls of the grain salad on the bottom. Using your hands pull apart the warm fish and spread evenly on top. Crack or use a knife to separate salmon skin into crisp size pieces before evenly spreading around salmon. Then, using a spoon, dollop the pomegranate sauce around the side and on top of the salmon.

SNAPSHOT

SERVES: **2**

- TIME
- HEALTHY
- SKILL

PROTEIN	FATS	CARBS
29.2g	28.7g (4.8g) saturated	21.9g (3.2g) sugars

per serve

STEP BY STEP GUIDE ▶

STEP BY STEP
CRISPY SKIN SALMON AND THREE GRAIN SALAD

SEAFOOD

WHOLE SNAPPER IN A TAMARIND SAUCE

I JUST LOVE SERVING WHOLE FISH TO THE TABLE BUT ONE OF THE BEST THINGS ABOUT THIS DISH IS YOU CAN PRE-MAKE THE SAUCE AND TAKE IT IN A TUPPERWARE CONTAINER TO A PICNIC SPOT OR DOWN TO THE BEACH. POUR THE SAUCE ON AND COOK IT ON A BBQ WHEREVER YOU ARE. OBVIOUSLY WE HAVE IT DOWN BY THE BEACH. DOESN'T GET MUCH BETTER THAN THAT.

INGREDIENTS

- 1 whole snapper, scaled & gutted
- 1 tbsp coconut oil
- 1 tsp mustard seeds
- 2 tsp chilli powder
- 1 tbsp turmeric, ground
- 2 tsp white pepper, ground
- 1 onion, finely chopped
- 2 garlic cloves, finely chopped
- 1 tbsp tamarind purée or water
- ½ cup (125ml) fish stock (page 26)
- ½ cup (125ml) coconut milk
- Fresh parsley, small handful of best leaves picked
- Fresh coriander, small handful of best leaves picked
- 1 cup brown rice
- 2 cups water

METHOD

Combine turmeric, chilli and white pepper and add 1 tbsp of water to make a paste, set aside.

Add the coconut oil to a frypan on medium to high heat. Once liquified add the mustard seeds and allow to fry for 30 seconds before adding the onion, garlic and ginger to brown.

Add the spice paste and mix through before adding the tamarind purée, turn the heat to medium and cook for 5 minutes. Add the fish stock and coconut milk and turn to low heat to infuse for 12 minutes.

Preheat the BBQ to medium-high heat and cover with the lid.

Lay out a sheet of aluminium foil on a bench and place the snapper in the centre. Curl up the edges to turn the sheet into a bowl.

Pour the tamarind sauce on top spreading evenly over the snapper.

Roll out another sheet of foil and wrap it over the top before putting onto the BBQ and cooking for 15 - 20 minutes. To test if it is cooked insert a knife into the thickest part of the fish then touch it to your bottom lip. If it is cold it is not yet cooked. You want it warm to hot. If its burning hot then, well, you do the math.

Meanwhile, put the rice in a saucepan with the water and cover with a lid on high heat. Bring to a boil and allow to simmer for 12 minutes, or until water is evaporated and rice has cooked through. Remove from heat.

Serve the whole fish at the table with the brown rice and spoon in the juices from the aluminium bowl.

SNAPSHOT

SERVES: **4**

TIME
HEALTHY
SKILL

PROTEIN	FATS	CARBS
31.3g	17.9g (11.9g) saturated	18.8g (1.9g) sugars

per serve

SEAFOOD

MUSSELS IN WHITE WINE

I WOULD NOT CALL THIS MY SIGNATURE DISH, BUT PROBABLY ONE THAT REPRESENTS ME AND THE BOYS A LOT. IT'S QUICK AND EASY AND WE LOVE TO HAVE IT DOWN BY THE BEACH WITH A COUPLE OF BEERS. BIGGEST WORRY IS IT CAN GET MESSY SO MAKE SURE IT'S NOT SOMETHING YOU EAT WITH YOUR EVENING ATTIRE ALREADY ON. ALTERNATIVELY YOU COULD USE A BIB - IT MAKES A GREAT ICE BREAKER!

INGREDIENTS

- 1 eshallot, finely chopped
- 1 garlic clove, finely chopped
- 1 tbsp olive or grapeseed oil
- ½ cup dry white wine
- ⅔ cup fish stock (page 26)
- 1kg mussels, cleaned and bearded
- Pinch of salt
- 4 tomatoes blitzed in a blender, or 1 tin
- ½ handful of parsley, roughly chopped; plus extra untouched leaves for garnish
- Juice of ½ lemon
- 2 tsp of tabasco or 4 good shakes

METHOD

On medium heat sweat the eshallots in oil for 5 minutes before adding the garlic, then cook for a further 4 - 5 minutes or until eshallots are translucent.

Add the tomatoes with a pinch of salt and stir for a minute before deglazing the saucepan with the white wine and fish stock. Turn the heat to low and reduce for 7 - 8 minutes.

Carefully place the muscles in and cover with a lid and cook for a further 3 - 4 minutes or until mussels begin to open.

Remove saucepan from heat add tabasco and parsley, along with lemon juice and give it a final stir before pouring into a serving dish. Top with fresh parsley leaves and don't forget a shell bin and finger bowl as things can get messy :)

Note: it is important to remove all of the beard around the mussels hinge. Just use your fingers to gently pull it away. Scrub the shell under running water. For fresh bread check out the next page. This is definitely something to be eaten on the balcony overlooking the water, or better yet, at the beach.

SNAPSHOT

SERVES: **4**

- TIME
- HEALTHY
- SKILL

PROTEIN	FATS	CARBS
23.1g	6.4g (11.5g) saturated	7.2g (2.8g) sugars

per serve

PRAWN & APPLE RICE PAPER ROLLS

IF YOU'RE LOOKING FOR SOMETHING LIGHT OVER LUNCH, THIS IS YOUR GO TO. YOU CAN EVEN SUBSTITUTE THE PRAWN FOR SOMETHING ELSE SUCH AS TOFU OR LEFTOVER CHICKEN. THE APPLE OFFERS A GREAT BURST OF SWEETNESS AND CRUNCH AS SOON AS YOU BITE IN.

INGREDIENTS

- 12 rice paper sheets
- 250g vermicelli rice noodles
- 12 cooked prawns, peeled
- 1 cucumber, julienned (thin strips)
- 1 carrot, julienned (thin strips)
- 1 green apple, cored & julienned (thin strips)
- 2 tsp sesame seeds
- Fresh mint, for serving
- Fresh coriander, for serving

Dipping Sauce

- 1 knob of ginger, peeled & finely chopped
- 1 garlic clove, finely chopped
- 1 long red chilli, finely chopped
- ½ handful mint, finely chopped
- ½ handful coriander, finely chopped
- 1 tsp palm sugar, grated
- 2 tbsp soy sauce
- 1 tsp rice wine vinegar
- Juice of ½ lime
- 2 tsp fish sauce
- ¼ cup water

METHOD

Cover the noodles with cold water and set aside for 15 minutes, then drain.

To make the sauce, combine all the ingredients in a bowl. I always endorse changing it to your liking so don't be afraid to alter what you think works better for you.

Submerge a rice paper roll in cold water for 12 seconds, then remove onto a tea towel, making sure not to let it fold in on itself as it will stick.

First add some noodles in a long fashion across the centre, then a few slices of carrots, cucumber and apple, top with two prawns before wrapping. To wrap, make a fold over the prawns, then fold in the sides before rolling the entire portion forward, this will keep it tight. Top with mint and coriander and serve with the dipping sauce.

See following pages to help you "wrap' your rolls.

SNAPSHOT   MAKES: 5

TIME	
HEALTHY	
SKILL	

PROTEIN	FATS	CARBS
8.7g	1.2g (0.2g) saturated	20.5g (2.4g) sugars

per serve

STEP BY STEP
PRAWN & APPLE RICE PAPER ROLLS

SEAFOOD

SEARED SCALLOPS
WITH APPLE AND FENNEL SALAD AND LEMON AIOLI

If you're having people over for dinner try this. If you have for some reason 'gone chef' and want to make an entree. It doesn't take much preparation and it leaves the guest wanting more and not feeling too full.

INGREDIENTS

- 12 scallops, roe removed
- 1 cucumber, julienned
- 1 granny smith apple, julienned
- 1 fennel bulb, core removed and shredded
- 2 egg yolks
- 1 tbsp Dijon mustard
- Pinch of salt
- Zest & juice of 1 lemon
- 100ml grapeseed/olive oil
- ½ handful flat Leaf parsley, finely chopped

METHOD

In a mixing bowl combine the Dijon mustard, egg yolks, salt and lemon zest with a whisk, then add a tiny amount of oil and whisk that in, gradually adding more of the oil until there is nothing left. Whisk in the lemon juice and set aside ready to serve.

Combine the apple, cucumber, parsley and fennel in a bowl, set aside.

For the scallops, put a pan on high heat. Once it is hot enough add one tablespoon of oil then add the scallops. Cook until they have a golden caramelisation to them, which should be no more than 1 - 2 minutes. Do not turn them over in the pan, instead turn over onto a separate plate or tray, allowing their residual heat to finish cooking themselves.

To serve, place the scallops on a plate and scatter the salad around before placing dollops of the lemon mayonnaise to finish.

SNAPSHOT

SERVES: **4**

TIME
HEALTHY
SKILL

PROTEIN	FATS	CARBS
6.0g	15.6g (1.0g) saturated	3.0g (2.6g) sugars

per serve

SEAFOOD

OVEN BAKED TROUT

YOU CAN HONESTLY GET THIS DONE, HAVE A SHOWER AND BE BACK TO COOK IT. WITH MINIMAL EFFORT ITS A GREAT WAY TO BEGIN COOKING FISH WHOLE. SO IF YOU WANT TO IMPRESS YOUR BOYFRIEND WHO LOVES HIS SEAFOOD YOU DEFINITELY HAVE TO HIT THIS ONE UP.

INGREDIENTS

- 1 whole trout, gutted & scaled
- 1 tbsp extra virgin olive oil
- 2 tsp salt
- 1 tsp white pepper, ground
- 1 knob of ginger, peeled and finely chopped
- 2 garlic cloves, finely chopped
- Juice & zest of 1 Lemon

METHOD

Preheat oven to 180°C.

In a bowl, add the garlic, ginger, lemon juice and olive oil and stir. On a chopping board, slice 4 - 5 little cuts, 1cm apart, on one side of the fish so you can see its flesh, this will be your top side.

Spoon the lemon sauce over each side of the fish and rub with your hands into the cuts. Remove one of the top racks from the oven and put it down on a heatproof surface. Place the fish on top of the hot rack, sprinkle with salt and pepper and place back in the oven, with a roasting tray directly beneath it to catch all the juices, for 12 - 15 minutes, or until cooked.

To test if it is cooked, insert a knife into the thickest part of the fish, then touch it to your bottom lip. If it is cold it is under. You want it warm to hot. If its burning hot then, well... you do the math.

Remove from the oven and spoon the reserved juices over the top of the fish. Serve whole at the table with sweet potato rosti.

SNAPSHOT

SERVES: **4**

TIME
HEALTHY
SKILL

PROTEIN	FATS	CARBS
38.4g	16.0g (3.4g) saturated	1.4g (0.6g) sugars

per serve

TUNA BUCKWHEAT TABBOULEH

TALK ABOUT BULK. MAKE THIS AT THE START OF THE WEEK AND YOU WILL NEVER HAVE A PROBLEM PREPARING LUNCHES AGAIN. IT'S FILLING AND GREAT ON THE POCKET TOO. MAKE SURE YOU RINSE THE BUCKWHEAT BEFORE COOKING TO GET RID OF THE EXCESS STARCH.

INGREDIENTS

- 1 ½ cups buckwheat, rinsed
- 180g tin tuna (I use springwater)
- 1 tomato, roughly chopped
- ½ bunch flat leaf parsley, finely chopped
- 1 regular spanish onion, finely chopped
- 1 cucumber, roughly chopped
- 1 long red chilli, finely sliced
- 1 avocado, cubed
- ½ cup walnuts
- ¼ cup extra virgin olive oil
- 1 tbsp Dijon mustard
- 1 clove garlic, finely chopped
- Juice of 1 lemon
- 3 sprigs thyme
- Pinch of salt

METHOD

Add the buckwheat and 3 cups of water to a saucepan on high heat. Cover and bring to the boil before turning to low and simmering for 12 - 15 minutes or until buckwheat is cooked through. Set aside to cool.

Combine the tomato, parsley, cucumber, onion, chilli, avocado and walnuts in a mixing bowl.

Carefully fold the buckwheat into the mixing bowl.

Drain the tuna and fold into the mix.

In a jar combine the oil, mustard, juice, thyme, salt and garlic. Close the lid and shake to combine. Alternatively mix the ingredients in a mixing bowl.

Bring the bowl to the table and pour over the thyme mustard, mix through and serve.

SNAPSHOT

SERVES: **6**

- TIME
- HEALTHY
- SKILL

PROTEIN	FATS	CARBS
12.2g	21.4g (3.0g) saturated	25.6g (2.6g) sugars

per serve

SEAFOOD MARINARA
WITH SWEET POTATO GNOCCHI

I LOVE MAKING GNOCCHI ESPECIALLY WHEN YOU FINISH IT IN THE FRYPAN SO THAT WHEN YOU BITE IN YOU HAVE THIS CRUNCHY OUTER SHELL WITH A SOFT CENTRE. THE SEAFOOD MARINARA IS GREAT FOR A FAMILY AND COST EFFECTIVE TOO, ESPECIALLY WHEN IT IS QUITE OFTEN ON SPECIAL.

INGREDIENTS

Seafood Marinara

- 5 roma tomatoes, halved
- 2 garlic cloves, finely chopped
- Salt
- 3 tbsp olive oil
- 1 onion, finely chopped
- ¼ cup black olives, pitted & roughly chopped
- 5 anchovies, finely chopped
- ¾ cup fish stock (page 26)
- ½ bunch flat leaf parsley, finely chopped
- ¼ cup lemon juice
- 500g seafood marinara mix

Gnocchi

- See page 31

METHOD

Follow Gnocchi recipe on page 31 before following the below.

Line an oven tray with baking paper and place the tomatoes cut side up on the tray. Sprinkle the tomatoes with garlic and a pinch of salt before drizzling over one tablespoon of olive oil. Put in the oven for 15 - 20 minutes, or until tomatoes are well shrivelled, then remove and put in a blender to blitz until smooth.

In a large frypan on medium heat add a tbsp of olive oil before adding the onions. Allow them to caramelise for 8 - 10 minutes, then stir in the blitzed roasted tomatoes and combine. Turn the heat to low and mix in the olives, anchovies and fish stock. Simmer for 30 minutes (you can do it for less time if you are in a hurry, just the flavour won't be as strong).

From the marinara mix first add the fish pieces into the sauce. Be sure to bury them and once they start to turn opaque, add the rest of the contents. Stir through for a final 2 minutes before removing from the heat, ready to serve.

To serve, spoon the sauce into the middle of a plate, ensuring to dish out the marinara mix evenly.

Top with the gnocchi and enjoy.

SNAPSHOT

SERVES: **4**

PROTEIN	FATS	CARBS
22.7g	9.7g (1.8g) saturated	4.6g (2.1g) sugars

per serve

STEP BY STEP
SEAFOOD MARINARA WITH SWEET POTATO GNOCCHI

SEAFOOD

SNAPPER WITH CREOLE SAUCE

A CREOLE SAUCE ORIGINATES FROM THE AMERICAS AND WITH THE ADDITION OF THE ONION RINGS I GUESS THE DISH IS COMPLETELY INSPIRED FROM THE USA. ALTHOUGH AMERICAN FOOD HAS BEEN STEREOTYPED TO NOT ALWAYS BE HEALTHY, THIS DISH OBVIOUSLY HASN'T BEEN EXPOSED ENOUGH AS IT IS FANTASTIC FOR YOU.

INGREDIENTS

- 1 red capsicum
- 1 tbsp pure olive oil
- 1 onion, sliced
- 1 garlic clove, finely chopped
- 1 tbsp tomato paste
- 1 tsp black peppercorns, ground
- ¼ cup fish stock (page 26), or water
- 1 handful parsley, finely chopped
- 1 handful chervil or fresh coriander, finely chopped
- 2 tbsp red wine vinegar
- 1 tbsp Worcestershire sauce
- 4 snapper fillets, skin on
- Salt

METHOD

If you have a gas top, using your tongs carefully roast the capsicum on all sides until skin is all dark and wrinkly, or, pre-heat your oven to 200°C, place the capsicum on a lined tray and cook in the oven for 15 - 20 minutes or until the skin is all shrivelled and wrinkly. Place the capsicum in a bowl and cover with cling wrap for 10 minutes so that the skin will peel away easily. Turn oven to 160°C.

Heat a medium size saucepan to medium heat and add the oil. Add the onions and cook until translucent, which should be 6 - 8 minutes. Add the garlic and cook until golden.

Meanwhile remove capsicum from bowl and using the sharp end of the knife peel away the skin, then remove the core, seeds and all the white membrane. Finely chop the flesh and set aside.

Add the tomato paste to the onion and allow to turn a rusty colour before stirring through the mix. Add in the capsicum and peppercorns before adding ¼ cup of fish stock or water. Cover with a lid and allow to simmer for 12 minutes.

For the fish, drizzle a little oil over the skin, sprinkle some salt and put in a frypan on medium heat skin side down. You want a nice sizzle, however, you don't want the fish to cook too quickly, this will come with practice. Cook the fish skin side down for about 3 - 4 minutes, have a look at the side of the fillet, when it starts to turn opaque ⅔ the way up, turn the fish over and put straight into the preheated oven for 2 - 3 minutes to finish cooking. If you don't have an ovenproof pan simply put the fish on a lined baking tray.

To finish the sauce off, remove the lid and add the worcestershire sauce, red wine, herbs and tabasco. Season with salt to taste, then put in a blender and pulse until smooth (you can still have it chunky if you want, but I prefer this one smooth).

To serve, spoon the creole sauce onto a plate and top with the snapper. I like to finish it with onion rings so check out page 22 for my recipe.

Note: the thickness of the fillet will obviously alter the cooking time. Sometimes you don't even need to turn the fish over and put in the oven, you can just put it simply onto a resting tray. This technique of cooking fish on one side is something I learnt from George.

SNAPSHOT

SERVES: **4**

- TIME
- HEALTHY
- SKILL

PROTEIN	FATS	CARBS
22.6g	5.3g (1.4g) saturated	2.9g (2.5g) sugars

per serve

VEGETARIAN

VEGETARIAN

If you asked me last year what I thought about having a meal without a solid protein, I wouldn't have been able to comprehend what you are asking. Sometimes the dominance of meat takes away the natural beauty of vegetables, fruit and seeds. Meat also contains a number of toxins. Obviously the more meat you consume the more toxins you will produce and too many can affect your body's cellular structure. Just like chocolate, having too much meat can be a bad thing. Therefore, with the inclusion of vegetarian meals in our intake it allows for a healthy balance, something that I, up until recently, struggled to come to terms with. As you are about to see though, not all dishes need meat, instead try some of these as they offer an amazing array of colour and flavour.

VEGETARIAN

BROCCOLI PESTO QUINOA SALAD

IF YOU HAVE A LOVE FOR YOUR PESTO, HERE IS A LITTLE TWEAK I LIKE TO DO WITH MINE. MAKE IT IN THIS DISH, BUT ALSO SUBSTITUTE IT FOR EVERY OTHER DISH THAT INCLUDES PESTO IN IT. IT STILL PACKS THAT ITALIAN PUNCH, JUST WITH A GREENER HEALTHIER OPTION. PERSONALLY I THINK IT IS A GREAT WAY TO GET YOUR KIDS TO EAT THEIR 'TREES'.

INGREDIENTS

- 1 cup of quinoa
- 1 broccoli head, cut into trees
- ½ handful basil, roughly chopped
- ¼ cup parmesan
- 1 garlic clove, roughly chopped
- ¼ cup toasted pine nuts
- 100ml olive oil
- ¼ cup toasted slivered almonds

METHOD

In a medium saucepan add the quinoa along with 1 ¾ cups of water. Bring to the boil and turn heat to a simmer for 10 - 12 minutes, or until quinoa opens.

Bring water to a boil in a medium saucepan, add the broccoli and blanch for 30 seconds before draining and running under cold water to prevent it from cooking any further.

In a small frypan, dry roast the pine nuts on high heat for 1 - 2 minutes to get a nice colour, remove and set aside.

In a food processor, add the pine nuts, garlic, basil, parmesan, salt and half the broccoli. Pulse and gradually add the olive oil. Do not process for too long as you still want a bit of texture. Spoon pesto into a bowl and squeeze over the lemon juice before mixing through.

Turn quinoa saucepan upside down and allow to freely pour out. If it is struggling to come out, be gentle and use a spoon to release. You don't want to mix the quinoa too much otherwise it will bruise and become stodgy.

This next part is up to you, spoon in 2 tbsp of the pesto mix and using a plastic spatula, gently fold the mix through. The amount of flavour of the pesto is down to how much you like it. I like a total of 2 ½ tbs plus a pinch of salt, then the rest of the pesto can be used for other meals.

Dry roast the slivered almonds for 1 - 2 minutes on high heat until golden.

Combine almonds with pesto quinoa mix, spoon onto a serving plate, top with remaining broccoli and finish with a squeeze of lemon and extra almonds.

SNAPSHOT

SERVES: 5

- TIME
- HEALTHY
- SKILL

PROTEIN	FATS	CARBS
8.5g	25.0g (3.2g) saturated	7.5g (0.8g) sugars

per serve

VEGETARIAN

RICOTTA, BEETROOT AND ZUCCHINI SLICE

IF YOU'RE LOOKING FOR A SLICE TO SHARE WITH SOME FRIENDS WHEN THEY COME OVER, OR AN ALTERNATIVE TO BREAKFAST OR BRUNCH WITH A CUP OF TEA, THEN TRY THIS OUT.

INGREDIENTS

- 3 zucchinis, grated
- 1 beetroot grated
- 1 tsp salt
- 3 eggs
- 1 tbsp Dijon mustard
- 1 garlic clove, finely chopped
- 500g ricotta
- ½ handful parsley, finely chopped
- ½ handful baby spinach
- Juice of ½ lemon

METHOD

Preheat oven to 160°C.

Place zucchini and beetroot in a colander with a pinch of salt for 15 - 20 minutes, allowing as much moisture to escape as possible. If you want to go that step further, you an dry them in a paper towel.

Whisk eggs and combine with mustard, parsley, spinach, lemon juice, garlic, and ricotta.

Layer a greased cake tin with zucchini, beetroot and egg mix until there is nothing left and cook in the oven for 40 - 50 minutes, or until golden on top.

Note: Beetroot stains, so use separate paper towels between vegetables and be sure not to get it on your clothes.

SNAPSHOT

SERVES: **8**

- TIME
- HEALTHY
- SKILL

PROTEIN	FATS	CARBS
12.5g	6.7g (3.5g) saturated	3.3g (3.3g) sugars

per serve

ITALIAN QUINOA SALAD WITH BASIL OIL

Although often referred to as a grain, quinoa is actually a seed. It is high in protein and much lower in carbohydrates compared to its grainier counterparts. I often substitute it for rice as its cooking method is pretty much the same.

INGREDIENTS

- 1 cup quinoa
- ¼ cup sundried tomatoes
- 100g Danish feta
- ¼ cup pine nuts

Dressing

- 1 bunch fresh basil
- Juice of ½ lemon
- Pinch of salt
- 100ml olive or grapeseed oil

METHOD

In a medium saucepan add the quinoa along with 1 ¾ cups of water. Bring to the boil, then turn heat down to a simmer for 10 - 12 minutes, or unto quinoa opens. Set aside to cool.

Bring a saucepan of water to the boil and drop ¾ of the basil leaves in for 20 seconds.

Drain in a colander and run under cold water for 1 minute so that it doesn't continue to change colour. Alternatively you can sit the colander in a bowl of iced water.

Put the basil leaves in a tea towel and roll it up. Ring out excess moisture by twisting, then place in a blender with the salt and lemon juice. Turn blender on and gradually add the oil until it all combines, set aside.

Dry roast the pine nuts in a small frypan on high heat for 1 - 2 minutes or until golden.

Turn quinoa saucepan upside down over a mixing bowl and allow to freely pour out. If it is struggling come out, be gentle and use a spoon to release. You don't want to mix the quinoa too much otherwise it will bruise and become stodgy.

Gently fold in tomatoes, pine nuts, feta and remaining basil into the quinoa.

Transfer to a serving dish, top with extra pine nuts and pour over the basil oil.

SNAPSHOT

SERVES: **5**

- TIME
- HEALTHY
- SKILL

PROTEIN	FATS	CARBS
12g	15.8g (3.2g) saturated	12.7g (3.9g) sugars

per serve

VEGETARIAN

TOFU, BUCKWHEAT AND CHICKPEA SALAD

THIS DISH WAS CREATED BASED ON WHAT I HAD IN MY FRIDGE AND PANTRY ONE DAY. OVER TIME I HAVE SLIGHTLY IMPROVED IT, BUT I GOT A GOOD KICK OUT OF HAVING MY OWN FORM OF MYSTERY BOX. IF YOU LOVE YOUR MEAT YOU HAVE TO GIVE THIS A GO. IT SHOWS YOU DON'T ALWAYS NEED MEAT FOR IT TO BE AN AMAZING DISH.

INGREDIENTS

- 1 cup buckwheat, rinsed
- 2 tbsp grapeseed oil
- 1 onion, sliced
- 2 garlic cloves, finely chopped
- ½ fennel bulb, sliced
- ½ cauliflower head
- ½ cup vegetable stock
- 150g chickpeas, drained
- 4 cardamom pods
- 1 tbsp coriander seeds
- Juice of ½ lemon
- 2 tsp of salt
- 250g firm tofu

METHOD

Add the buckwheat to a saucepan and add 2 cups of water. Bring it to the boil and turn heat to low to cook for 12 - 15 minutes, or until soft. Set aside.

Heat one tablespoon of oil in a deep frypan on medium heat and caramelise the onion for 8 minutes. Add the garlic and stir through before adding the fennel and cauliflower. Cook for five more minutes or until fennel and cauliflower turn golden.

In a small frypan dry roast the coriander seeds and cardamom pods for 1 minute before adding them to the vegetable mix.

Pour in your vegetable stock, turn heat to medium, season with salt and allow to simmer for 10 minutes, ensuring all liquid reduces down.

Carefully fold in your buckwheat and your chickpeas and allow to stand off the heat in a big mixing bowl.

In a frypan add remaining oil on high heat and cook the tofu on each side for 2 minutes until caramelised. Chop into cubes and add to the mixing bowl before finishing with a final squeeze of lemon juice and serving.

SNAPSHOT   SERVES: 4

TIME
HEALTHY
SKILL

PROTEIN	FATS	CARBS
14.5g	10.8g (1.4g) saturated	28.8g (3.7g) sugars

per serve

VEGETARIAN

SWEET POTATO ROSTI

THERE IS NO SURPRISE HOW MUCH I LOVE MY SWEET POTATO. I OFTEN PUT THIS DISH AT THE BOTTOM OF ANY SLOW COOKING DISH IN THE OVEN. IT ABSORBS THE JUICES AND BY BAKING YOU STILL GET A CRISPY EDGE THROUGH THE HEAT WITHOUT THE ADDED FAT FROM OIL. BETTER FOR YOUR BODY, EVEN BETTER FOR YOUR PALATE AND STOMACH. THIS RECIPE JUST SHOWS WHAT MINIMAL INGREDIENTS YOU NEED TO PUT A DISH TOGETHER.

INGREDIENTS

1 large sweet potato, grated (either by hand or using a food processor attachment)

1 tbsp cumin, ground (however you can use any spice you want)

1 tbsp coriander, ground

Good pinch of salt

2 tsp black pepper

2 tbsp extra virgin olive oil

METHOD

Preheat oven to 190°C.

Drizzle one tablespoon of olive oil into a roasting tray and then add in the sweet potato.

Combine the spices and sprinkle over the top of the sweet potato. Season with salt and pepper and drizzle with remaining olive oil.

Using tongs, stir the mixture around and put in the oven for 20 minutes, or until golden. I like to stir every 5 minutes to rotate the surface getting the most heat, however, if you want a crispy top, don't stir.

SNAPSHOT

SERVES: **5**

- TIME
- HEALTHY
- SKILL

PROTEIN	CARBS	FATS
3.6g	4.0g (0.5g) saturated	21.2g (8.2g) sugars

per serve

VEGETARIAN

BEETROOT AND SWEET POTATO CHIPS

BEETROOT IS ONE OF THE MANY ROOT VEGETABLES THAT OFFER A GREAT, NATURAL, SWEET TASTE AND SWEET POTATO CHIPS ARE ONE OF MY OLD TIME FAVOURITES. ENJOY THEM SEPARATE OR TOGETHER.

INGREDIENTS

Beetroot Chips

| 1 bunch of beetroot, peeled |
| 2 tbsp olive oil |
| 1 tsp of salt |

Sweet Potato Chips

| 1 large sweet potato, peeled |
| 2 tbsp olive oil |
| 1 tsp salt |

SNAPSHOT

Beetroot Chips — SERVES: **4**

TIME		
HEALTHY		
SKILL		

PROTEIN	FATS	CARBS
1.2g	4.9g (0.8g) saturated	5.5g (5.5g) sugars

per serve

Sweet potato chips — SERVES: **4**

TIME		
HEALTHY		
SKILL		

PROTEIN	FATS	CARBS
1.8g	4.4g (0.7g) saturated	13.4g (5.3g) sugars

per serve

METHOD

Beetroot Chips

Preheat oven to 180°C.

Chop off the ends of the beetroot and divide it in half down the centre to create two semi circle cylinders. Slice 2mm thick, resulting in semi circular chips.

Line a baking tray with baking paper and evenly spread the chips out, making sure they do not clump together. You may have to do more that one tray because if you overcrowd them it will effect their resulting texture.

Put in the oven to cook for 15 - 20 minutes. Keep an eye on them and turn if they are becoming too brown at the top.

Remove from oven, sprinkle with salt and allow to dry out for 10 minutes before serving on a platter.

Sweet potato chips

Preheat oven to 180°C.

Chop sweet potato into chip shapes and mix in a bowl with the oil.

Line a baking tray with baking paper and evenly spread the chips out, making sure they do not clump together. You may have to do more that one tray because if you overcrowd them it will effect their resulting texture

Put in the oven to cook for 25 - 30 minutes. Keep an eye on them and turn if they are becoming too brown at the top.

Remove from oven, sprinkle with salt and allow to dry out for 10 minutes. Because they have a lot of moisture they tend to be a bit soft, however if you pour them out onto a drying rack they become nice and crispy.

CHEATING

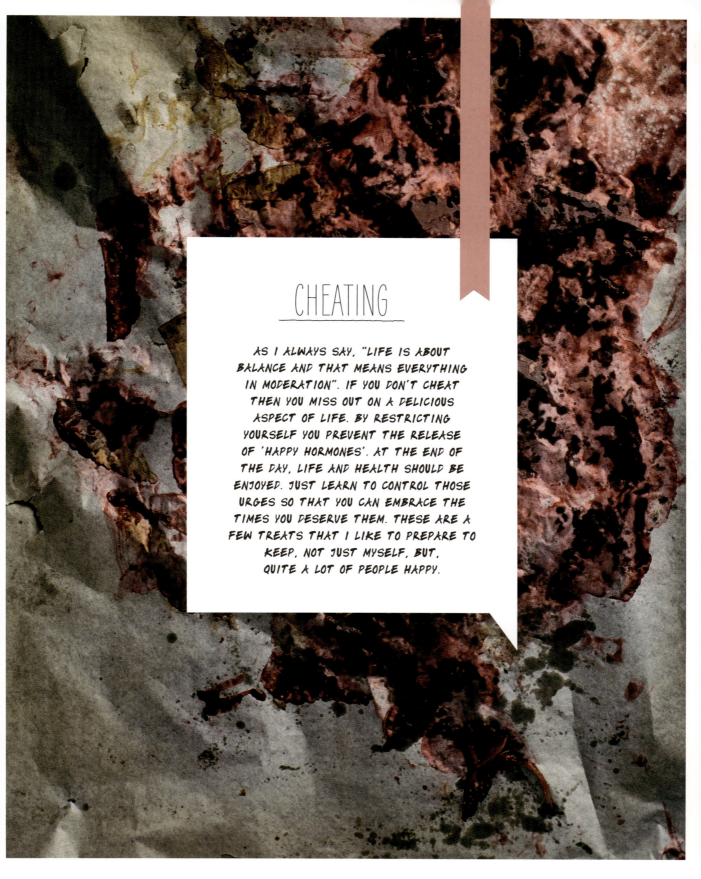

CHEATING

As I always say, "Life is about balance and that means everything in moderation". If you don't cheat then you miss out on a delicious aspect of life. By restricting yourself you prevent the release of 'happy hormones'. At the end of the day, life and health should be enjoyed. Just learn to control those urges so that you can embrace the times you deserve them. These are a few treats that I like to prepare to keep, not just myself, but, quite a lot of people happy.

COCONUT MILK COCO

I WORKED THIS ONE OUT WHEN I WAS CRAVING A HOT CHOCOLATE OVER WINTER. BECAUSE OF THE COCONUT MILK IT OFFERS A NUTTIER TEXTURE. ITS GREAT FOR A MOVIE NIGHT. MAKE SURE YOU GET A SOLID MUG TO WRAP YOUR HANDS AROUND THIS, ALONG WITH YOUR PAJAMAS TO ADD TO A PRETTY EPIC MID WEEK NIGHT IN.

INGREDIENTS

- 1 cup coconut milk
- 1 cup almond or dairy milk
- ½ cup cocoa nibs
- 1 tsp vanilla extract
- 1 tbsp maple syrup
- 1 tsp ground cinnamon or 3cm stick
- 1 tsp nutmeg

METHOD

Combine both milks in a saucepan and cover on high heat. Bring to the boil, then remove from the heat.

Add the cocoa nibs, maple syrup, cinnamon, nutmeg and vanilla extract and cover for 10 minutes allowing to infuse, stir occasionally.

If you want a smoother coco, pass through a sieve before ladling straight into a huggable mug, but I like a bit of texture so I include the nibs. Get involved!

SNAPSHOT

SERVES: **4**

TIME
HEALTHY
SKILL

PROTEIN	FATS	CARBS
7.4g	18.4g (11.9g) saturated	14.6g (9.9g) sugars

per serve

CHEATING

BUCKWHEAT PANCAKES
WITH APPLE & RHUBARB COMPOTE

I love these on my Sundays. Sometimes I make too much and because I like them fresh off the pan, hot, I store the batter until I am ready to use it. However you can cook it all and then reheat in the microwave.

INGREDIENTS

½ cup buckwheat flour

½ cup quinoa or plain flour

2 eggs

1 pinch salt

1 tbsp maple syrup or honey

1 ½ cups almond milk (or dairy milk)

½ tbsp coconut oil or olive oil

2 red apples, cored and cubed

1 bunch of rhubarb, cut into 3cm long strips

1 tsp allspice

1 tsp cinnamon

½ tsp vanilla extract

METHOD

Combine the flours and salt in a mixing bowl. In a separate bowl whisk the eggs and mix in the maple syrup and milk.

Add the wet to the dry and mix to a nice consistency before transferring to a pouring jug.

For the compote, add the oil to a small saucepan on medium heat and add the apple cubes. Sauté for 4 minutes before adding the rest of the ingredients along with two tablespoons of water. Bring to a boil before covering with a lid and simmering on low heat for 6 - 8 minutes. If you prefer a runny sauce, cook for longer and stir more constantly, but I like it so my apples are still cubed.

To cook the pancakes add oil to a hot pan and pour the mixture into the centre. Once the top reveals bubbles, carefully flip it over (this should take 2 - 3 minutes). Cook for a further minute on the other side. Leftover mixture can be kept for 2 days in the fridge.

Serve as a pancake stack with the compote on top and extra maple syrup if you're feeling devilish.

SNAPSHOT

SERVES: **5**

TIME
HEALTHY
SKILL

PROTEIN	FATS	CARBS
9.9g	13.7g (4.8g) saturated	22.5g (7.2g) sugars

per serve

PROTEIN BALLS

I HAVE A MASSIVE SWEET TOOTH AND WITHOUT THESE I WOULD DEFINITELY STRUGGLE A BIT. WITH THE INCLUSION OF PROTEIN, THESE BALLS ARE A GREAT SNACK OPTION, PARTICULARLY ON RESISTANCE DAYS.

INGREDIENTS

- 2 cups dates, pitted and roughly chopped
- ½ cup desiccated coconut, plus extra for finishing
- ½ cup LSA (Linseed, Sunflower Seed, Almond Meal)
- 1 scoop WPI Protein Powder
- ¼ cup cacao powder
- 1 tbsp organic peanut butter
- 80g walnuts, chopped
- 80g cashews, chopped (optional)
- 1 tsp ground cinnamon

METHOD

Soak the dates in a bowl in warm water for 15 minutes.

Drain the dates but reserve the soaking liquid. Put the dates in a blender or food processor and pulse until it resembles somewhat of a rough, dough consistency. If it is really dry gradually add some of the reserved soaking water.

Add the rest of the ingredients and mix until well combined. This should take 3 - 5 minutes.

Pick out portions of the mix and roll between your hands into mini golf ball size spheres. Repeat until all mix is used.

Finish by rolling the balls in the extra desiccated coconut.
You can then eat them straight away or store in a sealed container in the fridge.

Note: These are my favourite snack and they provide a substantial short burst of energy between work outs, not to mention the added protein for muscle repair.

As always, everything in moderation, and you will find these do have high GI sugar from the dates. So, when you make them, don't go overboard in consuming them and just try to have them on your more active days.

SNAPSHOT

SERVES: **10**

PROTEIN	FATS	CARBS
10.4g	12.4g (3.4g) saturated	7.8g (6.9g) sugars

per serve

SWEET STRAWBERRY
AND COCONUT MUFFINS

IF I SAID THESE HAD NO CONFECTIONARY SUGAR IN THEM YOU WOULDN'T KNOW IT. BY REMOVING THE MOISTURE FROM THE STRAWBERRIES YOU ENHANCE THEIR NATURAL SWEETENERS, MAKING THIS CHEAT LESS OF A TREAT BUT EVEN TASTIER.

INGREDIENTS

- ¾ punnet strawberries, topped and quartered
- ½ cup quinoa flakes (can also use oats)
- 1 ½ cups almond meal
- ¼ cup desiccated coconut
- ½ tsp chia seed
- 1 tsp baking powder
- 1 tsp salt
- 3 ½ tbsp maple syrup
- 2 tbsp olive oil
- 2 eggs
- ½ tsp vanilla extract
- ¼ cup cocoa nibs (optional)

METHOD

Preheat oven to 180°C.

Line a tray with baking paper and evenly spread the strawberries on top. Bake in the oven for 10 minutes, or until juicy and soft. Remove from oven and allow to cool.

In a mixing bowl, add the almond meal, quinoa flakes, chia seeds, coconut, salt and baking powder.

In another bowl combine the maple syrup, oil, vanilla extract and eggs

Mix the wet with the dry then fold in the cocoa nibs if using.

Scrunch up a 8 x 8cm piece of baking paper and unfold it to fit into the inside of a muffin tin. Repeat with remaining muffin holes. Alternatively you could use pre made muffin wrappers.

Spoon the mix into each tin ensuring there is ½cm gap from the edge to allow it to rise. Bake for 15 - 20 minutes or until a skewer comes out clean.

SNAPSHOT

SERVES: **6**

- TIME
- HEALTHY
- SKILL

PROTEIN	FATS	CARBS
8.3g	27.1g (5.2g) saturated	8.8g (8.8g) sugars

per serve

CHEATING

HOMEMADE TORTILLAS & TOSTADAS

MAKING YOUR OWN TORTILLAS IS HONESTLY THAT MUCH BETTER. THE FLAVOUR IS CLEANER, THERE ARE NO PRESERVATIVES AND IT'S PROBABLY ONE OF THE EASIEST THINGS TO DO. IF YOU DON'T HAVE A TORTILLA PRESS, SANDWICH BETWEEN TWO CHOPPING BOARDS LINED WITH FOIL, IT WORKS PRETTY MUCH THE SAME. MY TIP IS TO USE YOUR BODY WEIGHT WHEN PUSHING DOWN ;)

INGREDIENTS

- 1 cup corn meal (Masa Harina)
- 1 cup warm water
- Pinch of salt
- 1 tbsp olive, macadamia, or grapeseed oil

METHOD

To make the dough combine the Masa Harina, salt and water in a bowl. If you can handle it I usually boil the water in a kettle and add after allowing it to cool for two minutes. I find that the hotter it is, the better the texture of the dough becomes.

Continue to mix until it forms a workable dough. Remove from the bowl and begin to knead on a clean bench. Try to avoid adding more meal, but if it is really starting to stick, dust a little bit down. Knead until smooth and then cover with cling wrap and put aside for 30 minutes.

Remove from the cling wrap and divide into quarters with a knife. Using a rolling pin, carefully roll the dough to a flat circular shape. Once it gets to about 2cm thick, line the bench with baking paper, place the dough onto the paper and top with a another sheet. Using a chopping board, sandwich the dough to flatten further against the bench. Ideally you only want it to be a couple of millimeters thick. From here you can use a pastry cutter, or a mould and cut out circles to suit the size of your tortillas. I'm loving the Californian Mexican style and so I make them relatively small. Repeat with remaining quarters.

To cook tortillas simply add them to a hot frypan and cook without oil, cooking each side until golden brown.

To make tostadas, which give a nice crunch, add enough oil to a saucepan that will allow the tortillas to submerge. Once hot enough add tortillas and cook until golden and crispy. Remove onto a paper towel before serving.

Note: If you have a tortilla press, once removing form the cling film separate into golf ball size pieces and roll before lining the press with aluminium foil. Grease the press with a tiny bit of oil and place the tortilla ball in between. Holding the handle push down and then peel away to find your tortilla.

SNAPSHOT

Tortillas — SERVES: **15**

- TIME
- HEALTHY
- SKILL

PROTEIN	FATS	CARBS
2.4g	0.6g (0.1g) saturated	18.6g (0.2g) sugars

per serve

Tostadas — SERVES: **15**

- TIME
- HEALTHY
- SKILL

PROTEIN	FATS	CARBS
2.5g	11.5g (1.8g) saturated	18.6g (0.2g) sugars

per serve

CHEATING

FLOURLESS BANANA BREAD

THIS IS ONE OF THE FIRST DISHES THAT I REALLY CHALLENGED MYSELF TO TURN HEALTHIER. THE BOYS AND I WOULD LOVE GOING DOWN TO A LOCAL CAFE ON A SUNDAY MORNING TO GRAB A COFFEE AND BANANA BREAD ON OUR WAY TO CHECKING THE SURF. I WANTED TO FIND A WAY TO BE ABLE TO HAVE A SLICE MORE OFTEN WITHOUT THE OBVIOUS GLUTEN AND CONFECTIONARY SUGAR LOAD. MY VERSION HAS NO BUTTER, FLOUR OR ADDED CONFECTIONARY SUGAR AND IS GREAT FOR YOUR HAPPINESS. I LIKE TO PUT IT IN THE FRIDGE AND THEN TOAST IT WITH SOME RICOTTA.

INGREDIENTS

- 3 bananas
- 3 eggs, separated
- 2 tbsp honey or agave
- 2 tsp ground cinnamon
- 1 tsp allspice
- 1 cup sifted almond meal
- ¼ cup walnuts, crushed
- 1 tsp chia seeds

METHOD

Preheat oven to 160°C.

Halve a banana lengthways and set one aside. With the remaining 2 ½ bananas, thinly slice and then with the back of a fork mash the banana. You don't want it to be completely smooth but definitely well mashed.

Whisk the egg yolks with the honey 'til nice and smooth. Add the mashed banana, cinnamon, chia seeds and allspice and combine.

Using an electric mixer, whisk the egg whites until they reach soft peaks then add ⅓ of the yolk mix and using a plastic spatula, carefully fold the mixtures together ensuring not to release too much air. Once combined add another third of the yolk mix and repeat folding action before adding the final third.

Add the almond meal and carefully fold through.

Line a bread baking dish with baking paper (I scrunch it up so it fits into the corners) and pour the mix in.

Evenly distribute the walnuts about the mix and using a butter knife push them deep into the tray.

Carefully put the ½ banana slice, cut side up, across the top of the mix and sprinkle over extra chia seeds if you have them.

Put in the oven to cook for 18 - 22 minutes, or until it is golden brown and a skewer comes out clean.

SNAPSHOT

SERVES: **8**

- TIME
- HEALTHY
- SKILL

PROTEIN	CARBS	FATS
8.9g	18.1g (1.8g) saturated	17.9g (13.2g) sugars

per serve

THE HEALTHY COOK
INDEX

A

Agave
   Bircher with Raspberry Sauce 36
   Breakfast Smoothie 42
Almonds
   Almond Milk 14
   My Homemade Granola 46
Almonds, Slithered
   Broccoli Pesto Quinoa Salad 126
   Crispy Skin Salmon 98
Almond Meal
   Chicken Parmy 72, 73
   Corn Fritters with Avocado Salsa 44
   Flourless Banana Bread 152
   Onion Rings 20
   Sweet Strawberry & Coconut Muffins 148
Almond Milk
   Bircher with Raspberry Sauce 36
   Breakfast Smoothie 42
   Buckwheat Pancakes 144
   Choc Banana Protein Shake 38
   Coconut Milk Cocoa 142
   Country Chicken Sweet Potato Top Pie 80
   Corn Fritters with Avocado Salsa 44
   My Breakfast Frittata 40
   Sweet Potato Fritters 50
Anchovies
   Eye Fillet Steak 64
   Seafood Marinara 116
Apple, Green
   Green Smoothie 52
   Poached Salmon 96
   Prawn & Apple Rice Paper Rolls 106
   Seared Scallops 110
Apple, Red
   Buckwheat Pancakes 144
Avocado
   Corn Fritters with Avocado Salsa 44
   Green Smoothie 52
   Tuna Buckwheat Tabbouleh 114

B

Baby Spinach
   Juicy Chicken Breast 82
   Ricotta, Beetroot & Zucchini Slice 128
Banana
   Choc Banana Protein Shake 38
   Flourless Banana Bread 152
   Fruit Smoothie 48
Barley
   Crispy Skin Salmon 98
Basil, Fresh
   Broccoli Pesto Quinoa Salad 126
   Chicken Parmy 72
   Eye Fillet Steak 64
   Italian Quinoa Salad with Basil Oil 130
Beef
   Beef Tortillas with Kale Slaw 84
   Eye Fillet Steak 64
Beef Stock
   Beef Tortillas with Kale Slaw 84
Beetroot
   Beetroot & Sweet Potato Chips 136
   Ricotta, Beetroot & Zucchini Slice 128
Berries, frozen
   Breakfast Smoothie 42
   Fruit Smoothie 48
Broccoli, Head
   Broccoli Pesto Quinoa Salad 126
   Mustard & Peppercorn Roo 78
Brown Rice
   Whole Snapper in Tamarind Sauce 102
Buckwheat
   Crispy Skin Salmon 98
   Tofu, Buckwheat and Chickpea Salad 132
   Tuna Buckwheat Tabbouleh 114

Buckwheat Flour
   Beef Tortillas with Kale Slaw 84
   Buckwheat Pancakes 144
   Sweet Potato Gnocchi 30
Butter Beans
   Pull Apart Lamb 62

C

Cabbage, Red
   Beef Tortillas with Kale Slaw 84
Cabbage, White
   Beef Tortillas with Kale Slaw 84
Cacoa Powder
   Protein Balls 146
Capsicum, Red
   Mustard & Peppercorn Roo 78
   Snapper with Creole Sauce 120
Carrots, Dutch
   Lamb Cutlets with Macadamia Crust 74
Carrot, Regular
   Bouillabaisse 94
   Chicken Stock 28
   Country Chicken Sweet Potato Top Pie 80
   Mustard & Peppercorn Roo 78
   Prawn & Apple Rice Paper Rolls 106
Cashews, raw
   Breakfast Smoothie 42
   Green Masala 68
   My Homemade Granola 46
   Protein Balls 146
Cauliflower
   Tofu, Buckwheat and Chickpea Salad 132
Celery
   Bouillabaisse 94
   Chicken Stock 28
   Country Chicken Sweet Potato Top Pie 80
   Fish Stock 26
Chia Seeds

Bircher with Raspberry Sauce 36
Breakfast Smoothie 42
Choc Banana Protein Shake 38
Flourless Banana Bread 152
Fruit Smoothie 48
Green Smoothie 52
Sweet Strawberry & Coconut Muffins 148
Chickpeas
    Tofu, Buckwheat and Chickpea Salad 132
Chicken Breast
    Chicken Parmy 72
    Juicy Chicken Breast 82
Chicken Legs
    Smokey Chicken Legs 60
    Chicken Stock 28
    Country Chicken Sweet Potato Top Pie 80
    Green Masala 68
    Mustard & Peppercorn Roo 78
    Pull Apart Lamb 62
Chicken Thighs
    Sesame Satay Skewers 88
Chicken, Whole
    Green Masala 68
    Country Chicken Sweet Potato Top Pie 80
Chilli, Green Long
    Green Masala 68
Chilli, Red long
    Beef Tortillas with Kale Slaw 84
    Corn Fritters with Avocado Salsa 44
    Prawn & Apple Rice Paper Rolls 106
    Sesame Satay Skewers 88
    Tuna Buckwheat Tabbouleh 114
Chilli Powder
    Beef Tortillas with Kale Slaw 84
    Whole Snapper in Tamarind Sauce 102
Cinnamon, Ground
    Bircher with Raspberry Sauce 36
    Buckwheat Pancakes 144
    Choc Banana Protein Shake 38
    Coconut Milk Cocoa 142
    Flourless Banana Bread 152
    My Homemade Granola 46
    Protein Balls 146
    Smokey Chicken Legs 60
Cinnamon Stick
    Green Masala 68
Cocoa Nibs
    Coconut Milk Cocoa 142
    Sweet Strawberry & Coconut Muffins 148
Coconut, Dessicated
    Fruit Smoothie 48
    My Homemade Granola 46
    Protein Balls 146
    Sweet Strawberry & Coconut Muffins 148
Coconut Milk
    Coconut Milk Cocoa 142
    Green Masala 68
    Sesame Satay Skewers 88
    Whole Snapper in Tamarind Sauce 102
Coconut Oil
    Buckwheat Pancakes 144
    My Homemade Granola 46
    Whole Snapper in Tamarind Sauce 102
Coconut Water
    Fruit Smoothie 48
    Green Smoothie 52
Corn Tortillas
    Beef Tortillas with Kale Slaw 84
Cucumber, lebanese
    Poached Salmon 96
Cucumber, Regular
    Corn Fritters with Avocado Salsa 44
    Prawn & Apple Rice Paper Rolls 106
    Seared Scallops 110
    Tuna Buckwheat Tabbouleh 114
Cumin, ground
    Beef Tortillas with Kale Slaw 84
    Smokey Chicken Legs 60
    Sweet Potato Fritters 50
    Tofu, Buckwheat and Chickpea Salad 132
Cumin Seeds
    Butterflied Lamb 70
    Green Masala 68
    Lamb Cutlets with Macadamia Crust 74

D

Dates
    Protein Balls 146
Dijon Mustard
    Crispy Skin Salmon 98
    Mayonnaise 22
    Mustard & Peppercorn Roo 78
    Ricotta, Beetroot & Zucchini Slice 128
    Seared Scallops 110
    Tuna Buckwheat Tabbouleh 114

E

Eggs
    Buckwheat Pancakes 144
    Corn Fritters with Avocado Salsa 44
    Flourless Banana Bread 152
    My Breakfast Frittata 40
    Onion Rings 20
    Ricotta, Beetroot & Zucchini Slice 128
    Sweet Potato Fritters 50
    Sweet Strawberry & Coconut Muffins 148
Egg Yolk
    Crispy Skin Salmon 98
    Mayonnaise 22
    Seared Scallops 110
    Sweet Potato Gnocchi 30
Eshallot
    Mussels in White Wine 104

F

Fennel Bulb
    Fish Stock 26
    Poached Salmon 96
    Seared Scallops 110
    Tofu, Buckwheat and Chickpea Salad 132
Fennel Seeds
    Beef Tortillas with Kale Slaw 84
    Bouillabaisse 94
    Chicken Parmy 72
Fish Stock (26)
    Lamb Cutlets with Macadamia Crust 74
    Poached Salmon 96
Fish Sauce
    Green Masala 68
    Prawn & Apple Rice Paper Rolls 106
    Fish Stock 26
    Bouillabaisse 94
    Mussels in White Wine 104
    Poached Salmon 96
    Seafood Marinara 116

Snapper with Creole Sauce 120
Whole Snapper in Tamarind Sauce 102

G

Garam Masala (69)
    Green Masala 68
Ginger
    Green Masala 68
    Green Smoothie 52
    Oven Baked Trout 112
    Prawn & Apple Rice Paper Rolls 106
Grapeseed Oil
    Crispy Skin Salmon 98
    Mayonnaise 22
    Poached Salmon 96
    Seared Scallops 110
    Tofu, Buckwheat and Chickpea Salad 132

H

Hazelnuts
    Lamb Cutlets with Macadamia Crust 74
Honey
    Bircher with Raspberry Sauce 36, 37
    Breakfast Smoothie 42, 43
    Eye Fillet Steak 64-67
    Flourless Banana Bread 152, 153
    Juicy Chicken Breast 82, 83
    My Homemade Granola 46, 47
    Poached Salmon 96, 97
    Sesame Satay Skewers 88, 89

K

Kale
    Beef Tortillas with Kale Slaw 84
    Kale Chips 24
    Green Smoothie 52
Kangaroo Steaks
    Mustard & Peppercorn Roo 78

L

Lamb, Leg
    Butterflied Lamb 70
    Pull Apart Lamb 62
Lamb Rack
    Lamb Cutlets with Macadamia Crust 74

Leek
    Mustard & Peppercorn Roo 78
    My Breakfast Frittata 40
    Pull Apart Lamb 62
Lemongass
    Crispy Skin Salmon 98
    Poached Salmon 96
    Sesame Satay Skewers 88
Lentils
    Mustard & Peppercorn Roo 78
LSA (Linseed, Sunflower seeds, Almond Meal)
    Breakfast Smoothie 42
    Choc Banana Protein Shake 38
    Protein Balls 146

M

Macadamia
    Lamb Cutlets with Macadamia Crust 74
Maple Syrup
    Breakfast Smoothie 42
    Buckwheat Pancakes 144
    Coconut Milk Cocoa 142
    Sweet Potato Fritters 50
    Sweet Strawberry & Coconut Muffins 148
Masa Harina (Corn Meal)
    Homemade Tortillas & Tostadas 150
Mayonnaise (25)
    Beef Tortillas with Kale Slaw 84
    Middle Eastern Carrots (74)
Mushrooms
    My Breakfast Frittata 40
    Sweet Potato Fritters 50
Mussels
    Bouillabaisse 94
    Mussels in White Wine 104
Mustard Seeds
    Whole Snapper in Tamarind Sauce 102

O

Oats
    Bircher with Raspberry Sauce 36
    Breakfast Smoothie 42
    My Homemade Granola 46
Olives, Black
    Seafood Marinara 116

Onion, Brown
    Beef Tortillas with Kale Slaw 84
    Bouillabaisse 94
    Chicken Stock 28
    Country Chicken Sweet Potato Top Pie 80
    Fish Stock 26
    Green Masala 68
    Mustard & Peppercorn Roo 78
    My Breakfast Frittata 40
    Onion Rings 20
    Pull Apart Lamb 62
    Seafood Marinara 116
    Snapper with Creole Sauce 120
    Sweet Potato Fritters 50
    Tofu, Buckwheat and Chickpea Salad 132
    Whole Snapper in Tamarind Sauce 102
Onion, Spanish
    Corn Fritters with Avocado Salsa 44
    Tuna Buckwheat Tabbouleh 114

P

Palm Sugar
    Green Masala 68
    Prawn & Apple Rice Paper Rolls 106
Pancetta
    My Breakfast Frittata 40
    Sweet Potato Fritters 50
Parmesan
    Broccoli Pesto Quinoa Salad 126
Peanut Butter, Organic Crunchy
    Protein Balls 146
    Sesame Satay Skewers 88
Pepitas
    Chicken Parmy 72
    Corn Fritters with Avocado Salsa 44
Pineapple
    Fruit Smoothie 48
Pine Nuts
    Broccoli Pesto Quinoa Salad 126
    Italian Quinoa Salad with Basil Oil 130
Pommegranite
    Crispy Skin Salmon 98
Prawns
    Bouillabaisse 94
    Prawn & Apple Rice Paper Rolls 106

Protein Powder, Chocolate
    Choc Banana Protein Shake 38
    Protein Powder, WPI (Whey Protein Isolate)
    Protein Balls 146
Pumpkin, Butternut
    Juicy Chicken Breast 82

Q

Quinoa
    Broccoli Pesto Quinoa Salad 126
    Crispy Skin Salmon 98
    Juicy Chicken Breast 82
    Italian Quinoa Salad with Basil Oil 130
Quinoa Flakes
    Bircher with Raspberry Sauce 36
    My Homemade Granola 46
    Sweet Strawberry & Coconut Muffins 148
Quinoa Flour
    Buckwheat Pancakes 144

R

Raspberries, frozen
    Bircher with Raspberry Sauce 36
Red Wine Vinegar
    Chicken Parmy 72
    Snapper with Creole Sauce 120
Rhubarb
    Buckwheat Pancakes 144
    Rice, Brown Long Grain
    Green Masala 68
Ricotta
    Chicken Parmy 72
    Ricotta, Beetroot & Zucchini Slice 128

S

Salmon Fillet
    Crispy Skin Salmon 98
    Poached Salmon 96
    Salsa Verde 64
Scallops
    Seared Scallops 110
    Seafood Marinara Mix
    Seafood Marinara 116
Sesame Oil
    Sesame Satay Skewers 88
Snapper Fillets
    Snapper, Whole
    Whole Snapper in Tamarind Sauce 102
Spinach, Baby
    My Breakfast Frittata 40
Star Anise
    Bircher with Raspberry Sauce 36
Strawberries
    Sweet Strawberry & Coconut Muffins 148
Sumac
    Butterflied Lamb 70
    Lamb Cutlets with Macadamia Crust 74
Sweet Corn
    Corn Fritters with Avocado Salsa 44
Sweet Potato
    Country Chicken Sweet Potato Top Pie 80
    Sweet Potato Fritters 50
    Sweet Potato Gnocchi 30
    Sweet Potato Rosti 134

T

Tamarind Puree
    Whole Snapper in Tamarind Sauce 102
Tofu, Firm
    Tofu, Buckwheat and Chickpea Salad 132
Tomato
    Beef Tortillas with Kale Slaw 84
    Bouillabaisse 94
    Chicken Parmy 72
    Corn Fritters with Avocado Salsa 44
    Eye Fillet Steak 64
    Mussels in White Wine 104
    Seafood Marinara 116
    Sweet Potato Fritters 50
    Tuna Buckwheat Tabbouleh 114
Tomato, Sundried
    Italian Quinoa Salad with Basil Oil 130
Tomato Paste
    Beef Tortillas with Kale Slaw 84
    Chicken Parmy 72
    Snapper with Creole Sauce 120
Trout, Whole
    Oven Baked Trout 112
Tuna, tin
    Tuna Buckwheat Tabbouleh 114

V

Vanilla Extract
    Coconut Milk Cocoa 142
    Buckwheat Pancakes 144
    Sweet Strawberry & Coconut Muffins 148
Vanilla Pod
    Bircher with Raspberry Sauce 36
Vegetable Stock
    Tofu, Buckwheat and Chickpea Salad 132
Vermicelli Rice Noodles
    Prawn & Apple Rice Paper Rolls 106
Vinegar, Cider
    Lamb Cutlets with Macadamia Crust 74

W

Walnuts
    Bircher with Raspberry Sauce 36
    Flourless Banana Bread 152
    My Homemade Granola 46
    Protein Balls 146
    Poached Salmon 96
    Tuna Buckwheat Tabbouleh 114
White Wine, Dry
    Bouillabaisse 94
    Mussels in White Wine 104
White Wine Vinegar
    Country Chicken Sweet Potato Top Pie 80
    Fish Stock 26
    Mustard & Peppercorn Roo 78
    Sweet Potato Fritters 50
Wholegrain Mustard
    Juicy Chicken Breast 82
    Poached Salmon 96

Y

Yoghurt, Natural
    Green Masala 68
    Lamb Cutlets with Macadamia Crust 74

Z

Zucchini
    Ricotta, Beetroot & Zucchini Slice 128

THE HEALTHY COOK
WITH THANKS

It's amazing the amount of food sweat and tears that goes into these projects and without a special number of people and companies there is no way in the world this book would have been written, bound and read.

Firstly thanks go to the sponsor Global for providing us with best knife set and support. Everyone says a good tradesman never blames his tools but a cook definitely gets pardoned on this as life is that much easier with quality sharp knives.

I would also like to thank Freedom Furniture for supplying a number of plates and props. It's unbelievable how good an image looks with quality products. It's so important to have amazing colours and textures to generate the image you have in mind, so, without them, none of this would have been possible. Also, thanks to Catja and the girls from 'For Good' in Port Macquarie for helping us out with some additional styling items.

Thank you Phil Bolton for being patient and putting up with my poor punctuation, your an amazing editor.

To Todd and the kitchen at LV's, thank you for being so supportive and letting me into your kitchen to make a mess – best restaurant in Port Macquarie!!!

To the Edwards family, thank you also for letting us into your home for the weekend. The passion you hold for food and cooking is something I hope my family will mirror one day.

To Michael, thank you for putting up with my direction and also shooting over 10,000 photos over 5 days.
I feel sorry for your computer, you're a true legend.

To Scott, the coach. Whether you know it or not, you are one of the main reasons I could put this project together. Without your friendship, ongoing support and encouragement, my dream would take even more years to be achieved. Our business would not be the same without you so lets keep aiming high.

A very special thanks to an amazing stylist in Madi Coppock. She truly has a tremendous eye and whenever I have something I want in my mind portrayed into an image, she understands it and also makes it that much better. She has been a tremendous support throughout this book and, to be honest, her job entailed much more than a stylist.

To Louise, Jordyn and Jesse, thank you for allowing me to take over your kitchen for 5 days, the fact you didn't complain or whinge is amazing, something I would have done if I had someone blocking my fridge. Thank you for all the help and support in setting up, administration roles, photography and bringing an amazing attitude to each day.

To Jay, well dude, you are something else. I know you are the graphic designer for this but you also acted like a producer, working your butt off to make deadlines. You are a magician and I am pretty sure you had your hand in every production aspect on this. Can't wait to get started on the next one.

To Dale & Emma, your guidance is remarkable and it is through people like yourself that gives many of us hope. You inspire and aid whenever it is needed.

To my Churchill family, where would I be without your constant support and love. My journey and passion through food would never have started without you. If it wasn't for our weekly cooking roster I would not be the person I am today.

Finally, to you the foodie's, fans and readers. Without any of you none of this would be possible. It is my passion to want to inspire you that makes me determined to make a difference and so without your presence I simply would not be so driven.

The Healthy Cook
By Dan Churchill
Copyright © 2013 Dan Churchill

www.danielchurchill.com.au
www.facebook.com/danthehealthycook

Design by Jay Beaumont
www.clickinc.com.au

All rights reserved. No part of this book may be reproduced or transmitted by any person or entity, in any form, or by any means, electronic or mechanical, including photocopying, recording, scanning, or by any information storage and retrieval system, without prior permission in writing from the publisher.

ISBN Number 978-0-9923501-0-9

Printed in China.

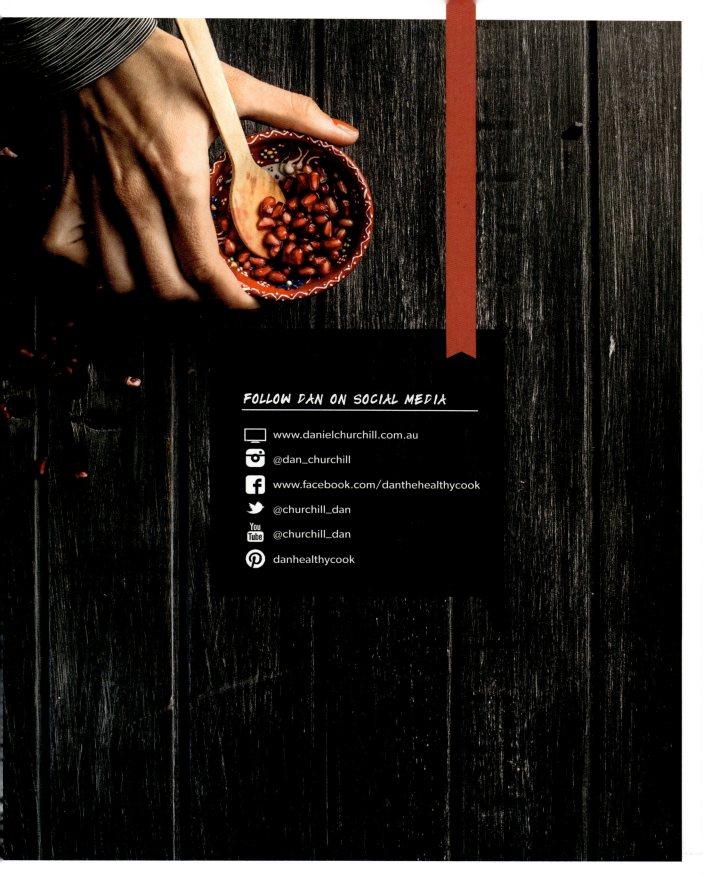

FOLLOW DAN ON SOCIAL MEDIA

- www.danielchurchill.com.au
- @dan_churchill
- www.facebook.com/danthehealthycook
- @churchill_dan
- @churchill_dan
- danhealthycook